BERLITZ®

CALIFORNIA

D0596471

- A  in the text denotes a highly recommended sight
- A complete A–Z of practical information starts on p.117
- Extensive mapping throughout: on cover flaps and in text

Printed in Switzerland by Weber SA, Bienne.

1st edition (1994/1995)

Although we make every effort to ensure the accuracy of the information in this guide, changes do occur. If you have any new information, suggestions or corrections to contribute, we would like to hear from you. Please write to Berlitz Publishing at the above address.

Text:	Neil Wilson
Editors:	Jane Middleton, Claire Evans Calder
Photography:	Doug Traverso
Layout:	Cristina Silva
Cartography:	Falk-Verlag, Hamburg

Thanks to: the San Francisco Visitor Information Center, the Los Angeles Convention and Visitors Bureau and the San Diego Visitor Information Center for their invaluable help in the preparation of this guide.

Cover photograph: Golden Gate Bridge, San Francisco

CONTENTS

California and the Californians

California has always been a magnet for people in search of a new beginning. From the earliest Spanish explorers and Mexican settlers, wagon trains and gold prospectors, to the Okies, hippies and the aspiring film stars, this golden land on the western edge of the continent has attracted dreamers in search of fame, fortune, freedom and opportunity.

A land blessed with sunshine and sea, fertile valleys and beautiful mountains, California is for many the ultimate fantasy land. It's no accident that this is the chosen home of the American film industry. California can offer every imaginable setting for a story, or a dream – the Swiss Alps, the Sahara Desert, an English meadow, the African jungle – and all can be found just a few hours' drive from Hollywood. Of course, what isn't already there – a Roman forum or an Egyptian pyramid – can be built in a few days.

There are some who believe it's not too pretentious to claim that California is, for better or worse, at the leading edge of human evolution. For the last couple of million years, they say, this is where we've been heading. Mankind has evolved from hunting through agriculture to industry, and on to the post-industrial age of leisure, coping with adversity so successfully that they can finally enjoy a life of ease and tranquillity. Well, at least in California they can.

This is not to say, however, that California is a place where everyone idles the hours away beside the pool. The state is a powerhouse of energy and activity, a hotbed of innovation. Its prosperity is truly overwhelming – it began with the gold prospectors of the Sierras, and spread across the great Central Valley with the gigantic combines of agribusiness, and then on to the coast where today's big money comes from oil, aerospace and computers. Californians are more than **5** prepared to work, and work hard, but they can't wait to get back to the beach, the tennis court or the swimming pool, to catch some surf in the Pacific, or hike the trails of Yosemite. Life here can be so much fun that it's positively exhausting. After a couple of weeks, you'll be almost glad to get back to a spell of homespun humdrum.

In their constant quest for novelty, Californians happily accept their role as America's last pioneers. From mountain bikes, windsurfers, roller disco and skateboards to microcomputers, 'flower power', theme parks, and New Age mysticism – it all originates, flourishes and finally fizzles out in California, while the rest of the world watches and wonders, and, more often than not, follows suit.

Denim jeans began their life in San Francisco, originally to withstand the wear and tear of the 1849 Gold Rush, and then became the universal fashion statement of the late 20th century. Bikinis, too, put in their first appearance on the golden beaches of California.

California might not have invented the automobile, but it was the first place to embrace it as a way of life. Los Angeles produced not only the first petrol (gas) station, but also the first supermarket, the car's own grocery store where customers could at last take away more than they could carry. There then followed, as a matter of course, the drive-in cinema, drive-in restaurant, drive-in bank, drive-in church, and even the drive-in funeral parlour. Since the motor caravan, known as an RV (recreational vehicle), became popular during the seventies, it's now possible to live in California and never leave your vehicle. Indeed, the story goes that some years ago a Los Angeles car dealer was buried along with his Cadillac.

With a population of about 29 million inhabitants, California is America's most populous state, and third largest in area after Alaska and Texas. Its per capita income is one of the highest in the world, and the state's economy – separate from the rest of the USA –

6

ranks seventh in the world. It also boasts the world's highest vehicle/inhabitant ratio – two cars for every three Californians. The expressway system is immense, but still it struggles to cope – traffic conditions on the freeways, as they're called

The Malibu equivalent of an afternoon stroll – surfers enjoy the waves at Surfrider Beach.

here, is as pervasive a topic of conversation as the weather in the United Kingdom or good wines in France.

However, it would be wrong to conclude that Californians are irredeemably materialistic. Hand in hand with the pursuit of pleasure goes a quite pronounced obsession with spirituality. Each religious sect and denomination you can think of is represented in California, as well as a variety of esoteric

An efficient highway system links the skyscrapers of downtown LA to the mountain playground of the Sierra Nevada.

cults, such as the Moonies and Scientology, and countless homespun variations on the ancient faiths of Asia. When tired of borrowing and adapting from other faiths, Californians have not hesitated to simply invent their own. Nevertheless, California is a remarkably conservative state. It is a nursery for new ideas, but by and large it prefers the tried and tested – the majority of Californians are conventional Christians, Jews or atheists.

Ethnically, the mix is predominantly Anglo-Saxon, but **8** Mexicans are also prominent in Los Angeles – one-third of the US's Mexican-Americans, or *chicanos*, live in California – and Italians and Irish in San Francisco. Since World War II, blacks have moved to California from the southern states in appreciable numbers, mostly to larger cities. The Japanese and Chinese have their most thriving communities in San Francisco, and in recent years large numbers of immigrants from Korea, Vietnam, Hong Kong and the Philippines have further increased California's Asian population. The original inhabitants, the Indians, or Native Americans, now number about 198,000, around two-thirds of the figure when the first Spanish settlers arrived in 1769.

California's most enthusiastic tourists are Californians. If you want to know where to go, follow the locals – nobody is more appreciative of the natural beauty of the state than the people who live here. In addition to the attraction of California's economic prosperity, people have moved here because of the beaches, mountains, the forests and the lakes. San Francisco's severe hills and cramped housing, not to mention the constant threat of earthquakes have done nothing to diminish the appeal of its outstanding natural beauty.

Perhaps it is the landscape itself that inspires this prosperous, forward-looking society. The delightful wine-producing valleys of the north as well as the fertile soils of the great Central Valley, where oranges, avocados, peaches and figs grow bigger and better than anywhere else, are Californian symbols of plenty. The mountains of the Sierra Nevada are a naturalist's paradise, where the soaring redwood groves of the Sequoia and Kings Canyon National Parks offer a peaceful retreat, far from the congested freeways of the city. At the heart of the mountains lies the splendour of Yosemite Valley, a natural cathedral which instils that hazy mysticism and sense of spirituality so characteristic of California. In addition, the vast and variegated desert landscapes of Mojave and Death Valley, with their wide and unbounded horizons, reflect the unbounded imagination of California, inspiring that real sense of potential, the feeling that here anything is possible, which continues to draw pioneers, visionaries and dreamers to this wonderful Golden State.

A Brief History

The first wave of Californian immigrants came somewhere between 20,000 and 35,000 years ago – wandering Asiatic tribes who entered the American continent via the Bering Strait, which at that time was dry land, or perhaps covered in ice. In the succeeding centuries, their descendants continued to push south and east, and eventually spread out to people the whole of the continent from Alaska to Patagonia. The tribes who decided to settle in what is now California were fortunate in their choice of homeland. The climate was very pleasant, and food was sufficiently plentiful for them to avoid the constant warfare that plagued many tribes elsewhere in the Americas.

The Indian tribes lived in harmony with nature. Anticipating 1960s flower children seeking drug-induced enlightenment, medicine men drank the juice of the jimson weed to provoke revelatory hallucinations. However, not even their wildest visions prepared them for the arrival of bearded men armed with swords and crossbows, in whose wake the Indian population plummeted from a peak of 275,000 to a mere 16,000 at the start of the 20th century.

The Spanish Missions

The first Europeans landed on the Californian coast in the 16th century – Spanish explorers in search of gold, seeking to extend their Mexican empire northward. In 1542 Juan Rodríguez Cabrillo, a Portuguese mariner in the employ of the Viceroy of Mexico, landed at Point Loma, at the mouth of San Diego harbour. He sailed on past the 'Bay of Smokes' (San Pedro in present-day Los Angeles), and on through the Santa Barbara Channel. During a scuffle with Indians he broke his leg and contracted gangrene, which was to prove fatal, but his crew pushed on as far as Oregon. They found few good harbours, however, and no sign of gold, and had to return empty-handed.

In 1579 England's Francis Drake, during the round-the-world trip that earned him his knighthood, took a break from harrying Spanish treasure galleons and stopped for repairs at Point Reyes (Drake's Bay, just north of San Francisco). He claimed the whole coastal territory for Queen Elizabeth I, but England was being kept busy with other concerns and no attempt was made to settle the new territory.

In 1769 the Spanish began to settle in California, establishing a string of military garrisons (*presidios*) and religious missions. The first was built in San Diego in 1769, and then in 1770 Monterey was founded as capital of Alta (Upper) California. The long peninsula of Baja (Lower) California remained separate and ultimately became part of Mexico.

These early missionaries, who were led by the Franciscan friar Junípero Serra, were all tough and courageous men, who faced hunger and hardship when their first agricultural efforts failed. Their plan was to convert the Indians to Christianity, teach them European farming methods as well as other skills and crafts, and then return the land to them

The art of California's native tribes is preserved in LA's Southwest Museum.

EL CAMINO REAL
MISSION SANTA BARBARA
FOUNDED DECEMBER 4, 1786
MISSION SAN BUENA VENTURA 30
MISSION SANTA INEZ 48
AUTO CLUB OF SO. CAL.

*F*ather Junípero Serra (right) began the missions which led the early Spanish colonization.

before moving on to set up another mission somewhere else.

The missionaries remained active well into the 19th century, and encouraged Spanish settlers by establishing California's first towns, the *pueblos*. By 1804 they had created a chain of 21 missions which, stretched all the way from San Diego north to Sonoma.

Two notable localities were first settled during this period. In 1776 a *presidio* and a mission were built near the mouth of the beautiful bay discovered by Gaspar de Portolá in 1769 – it was named the Misión San Francisco de Asís.

The first two *pueblos* to be founded were the Pueblo de San Jose de Guadalupe, near San Francisco, as well as in the south El Pueblo de Nuestra Señora la Reina de los Angeles del Río de Porciúncula – 'The Town of Our Lady the Queen of the Angels by the River Porciúncula'. Founded in 1781 with a total of 46 settlers, mostly Indians, in time its name was mercifully shortened to – you guessed it, Los Angeles.

At this time, California was not considered a particularly attractive proposition by its Spanish overlords. Distracted by the Napoleonic wars raging in Europe, they finally abandoned the territory when Mexico declared its independence in 1821.

The Mexicans

As far as California was concerned, the Mexican takeover was practically bloodless. In fact, California's 26 years of rather loose Mexican administration (1822-48) were characterized by a series of bloodless revolutions. The governorship at Monterey changed hands 11 times in a period of 5 years, not counting three governors whom Mexico City had dared to impose and whose authority was then completely ignored. There was some half-hearted fighting between northerners and southerners for control of the property and lands left by the Spanish missionaries, half of which was meant to be returned to the Indians but it never happened.

California grew into a territory with just one industry – cattle ranching, for the sale of cowhide and tallow. In the meantime, the old crafts were abandoned and California started to earn a reputation as a place of leisure. Richard Dana, a Massachusetts lawyer who visited California in the 1840s, was appalled by the sloth and wastefulness of its inhabitants. Nevertheless, he commented rather astutely: 'In the hands of an enterprising people, what a country this might be.'

The American Pioneers

The first Americans to come to California from the eastern states were Boston fur traders taking the Cape Horn route at the end of the 18th century.

They didn't stay for long, but gradually other traders and fur trappers began to arrive overland through Utah, Nevada, Arizona and New Mexico, settling only in small numbers, until the famous covered wagons began their heroic treks of the 1840s. The hardships they suffered in the Sierra Nevada mountains, Death Valley and the Mojave Desert became the stuff of Californian legend, the most tragic being the fate of 87 pioneers who set out from Illinois in 1846. While attempting to cross the Sierra Nevada, George Donner's wagon train became snowed in, and from November until February was stuck high in the mountains north of Lake Tahoe, at a point now known as the Donner Pass. Just 47 people survived, and then only by resorting to cannibalism.

Just simple farmers seeking a place in the sun to work a piece of land, these pioneers came at a time when territorial expansion was much in vogue – the French in the Pacific and Algeria, the British in Africa and the Far East. The United States was eager to get in on the act and so, during the war with Mexico over the annexation of Texas, California was suddenly regarded as a useful addition to the spoils. United States forces recaptured Los Angeles in 1847, and the Mexicans capitulated at Cahuenga. A treaty of American annexation of California was signed on 2 February 1848. Meanwhile, unknown to the American and Mexican signatories, gold had been found in the Sierra Nevada foothills only nine days earlier.

The Gold Rush

The find that caught the whole world's imagination was made by one James Wilson Marshall, a carpenter, at John Sutter's sawmill on the American River at Coloma, which lies midway between Sacramento and Lake Tahoe. He had found flakes of 23-carat gold in the river gravel and, in the following year alone, 6,000 prospectors poured in from Hawaii, Oregon, Utah, Mexico, Peru and Chile, and proceeded to

*T*wenty-mule teams once hauled wagonloads of ore from the mines of Death Valley.

dig up $10 million worth of the precious metal. In 1849 the Gold Rush really began, with 40,000 fortune hunters from all parts of North and South America scrabbling for the $30 million worth of gold.

By 1852, at the peak of the mining boom, there were over 100,000 prospectors in the region, all fiercely individualistic, and working away at their personal, private stakes rather than banding together in organized syndicates.

There was also another fortune to be made – this time from the service industries – and San Francisco, home of the banks and manufacturers **15** of mining equipment, began to grow into a metropolis. All kinds of conmen and hustlers flocked in to part the diggers from their gold dust. Manuals such as *The Emigrant's Guide to the Gold Mines* became instant bestsellers – 25 cents for 30 pages, half price without the map, which was hopelessly inaccurate anyway. One of the more enduring spin-offs of the Gold Rush was the hard-wearing work trousers sold by the Bavarian immigrant and entrepreneur, Levi Strauss. Originally made from tent canvas, and later from the twill-weave cotton known as denim, Levi's jeans are now world famous.

Lured by the promise of increased federal revenues from the newly discovered gold, the US Congress admitted California as the 31st state of the Union in 1850.

Statehood

The early years of statehood were marked by a rough and ready kind of justice. In the absence of a well-established judiciary or organized police force, law and order was enforced by vigilantes, and summary hanging was the usual sentence. Life was not easy for the remaining Mexicans and Indian inhabitants, nor indeed the immigrant Chinese. Mexicans were excluded from the mining bonanza by a hefty 'foreigner's tax', and most of them were forced to leave. The Chinese arrived in the wake of the great Taiping Rebellion of 1851, seeking security and prosperity in what they were told were California's 'Golden Mountains'. They suffered both exploitation by Chinese entrepreneurs, who used them as indentured labour, and discriminatory taxation by the state legislature. The worst-treated, however, were the native Indians, whose numbers dwindled rapidly not only as a result of disease and malnutrition but also because of systematic massacres in the 1850s by Californian militia.

In 1859 the discovery of silver (the Comstock Lode in western Nevada) caused a Silver Rush in the reverse direction, with the mining being organized almost completely from California. As the state's economy expanded, its major priority became a transcontinental railway to connect it to the eastern markets. Engineer Theodore Judah defied all the experts by plotting a railway link between Sacramento and the East, passing right through the heart of the Sierra Nevada and the Rocky Mountains. He managed to sell his idea to a San Francisco consortium that became known as the Central Pacific's 'Big Four' – Mark Hopkins, Collis Huntington, Charles Crocker and Leland Stanford – names that continue to echo in both the streets and institutions of present-day California.

The railroad project transformed the Big Four's personal assets of $100,000 in 1861 into a fortune of $200 million. The line, which linked up with the Union Pacific at Promontory, Utah in 1869, was built under the most hazardous conditions, using poorly paid Chinese labourers who worked suspended in wicker baskets over sheer cliffs to hack a tenuous cutting through the steep passes of the Sierras.

The Great Earthquake

The more devout Californians were convinced God was punishing San Francisco for its gold lust and sinfulness when an earthquake, registering 8.25 on the Richter Scale, struck the city at 5.13am on 18 April 1906. The initial quake wiped out about 5,000 buildings, but the great fire that followed destroyed most of the city. With the water mains shattered, the City Fire Department could do nothing to stop the fire from spreading out of control.

The earthquake and fire together caused 452 deaths, according to official estimates, but the imposition of martial law by Mayor Schmitz (without authorization) resulted in up to 100 more dead in summary executions for looting or refusing to help the firefighters. The performance of the military was less than exemplary – as Chinatown burned, it was looted by the National Guardsmen sent to protect it. **17**

Reform, Progress and Oil

The San Francisco earthquake helped to focus the nation's attention on the graft and corruption that ran right through the heart of Californian society. The federal prosecution succeeded in jailing only a handful of the principals involved, but the publicity was enough to make the concept of 'reform' a popular one.

The reform movement, intent on breaking the political power of the big corporations, attacked corrupt practices in

administration, public finances and banking, but did nothing to oppose the businessmen's traditional resistance to unions and more liberal labour laws. There was also a campaign of official discrimination against Chinese and Japanese immigrants, excluding them from owning land and preventing further immigration.

These discriminatory practices were perhaps sadly inevitable in a young state eager to find and assert its own identity. Its burgeoning prosperity seemed too good to be true. All kinds of useful produce grew large and lush in California's fertile, irrigated soil, but the most financially profitable thing to come out of the Californian earth was oil.

Drilling had begun in the 1860s but didn't take off until 1892. By the 1920s, the derricks of the Standard, Union and Shell oil companies had

Oil was the fuel behind California's economic boom in the early 20th century.

sprouted all over the Los Angeles basin. In that one decade, the state's oil revenues were $2,500 million, $500 million more than all the gold that the Sierras produced in a century.

Sunny, oil-rich Los Angeles was therefore the perfect place for the car to emerge as an everyday household accessory. From 1920 to 1930 LA's population more than doubled, and the number of private cars increased fivefold. Noting the central position of the 'pursuit of happiness' in America's Declaration of Independence, the *Los Angeles Times* asked in 1926: 'How can one pursue happiness by any swifter and surer means than by the use of the automobile?'

Hollywood

If you didn't feel like pursuing happiness in a car, you could sit in the dark and dream about it in the cinema instead. The booming popularity of this new entertainment form meant that the film production companies, based originally in the East, had to find a place where they could shoot outdoors for 52 weeks a year. They finally settled in a suburb of Los Angeles – Hollywood – where there was guaranteed sunshine all the year round and, within easy reach of the new studios, deserts and mountains, as well as beaches, rivers, forests, and islands which could double for the Wild West, the Holy Land, the Mediterranean – wherever. In addition, taxes were lower than in New York, labour was cheap and plentiful, and land and property prices were low, allowing the film companies to buy up vast tracts of prime real estate for their studios and back-lots.

Hollywood soon became a Mecca for dreamers. Somewhat dubious 'talent schools' sprang up, catering to small-town girls who hoped to emulate film stars such as Mary Pickford. If they didn't make it as actresses, the 'schools' turned them into call girls for the producers, and in 1922 the lurid rape trial of comic Fatty Arbuckle highlighted Hollywood's decadent lifestyle of fast cars, bootleg whisky and **19** drugs. The immediate reaction was the imposition of the Hays Office code of morals, which decreed that in all Hollywood films sin must be punished – it could be shown in detail, but it must always be punished.

The industry cashed in on the boom years of the 1920s. Hollywood Boulevard introduced lavishly exotic Chinese and Egyptian-style cinemas, and film stars built homes to match in Beverly Hills, the most famous being the Pickfair mansion, a hunting lodge which Douglas Fairbanks and Mary Pickford turned into a honeymoon estate. However, in spite of the glamour, Hollywood's rather seedy image persisted. Boarding houses in Los Angeles sometimes advertised 'Rooms for rent – no dogs or actors allowed'.

Depression and Boom

The Great Depression hit California hard. Income from agriculture dropped by 50 percent between 1929 and 1932 and one-fifth of the state's population was on public relief. California managed to weather the downturn better than the rest of the country, however, and became a magnet for dispossessed refugees from the Dustbowl of the Midwest. 'Okies', as they were known, packed their families and belongings into rickety cars and trucks to make the epic voyage West to find work in the farms and orchards of California. Their tale of hardship, pride, bitterness and exploitation is graphically recorded in the Pulitzer Prize-winning novel *The Grapes of Wrath*, by Californian writer John Steinbeck.

Then came World War II, bringing with it an enormous boom for the state's beleaguered economy, with the US federal government spending $35,000 million in California. Overnight, ships and planes became the state's most important products. Manufacturers such as Douglas, Lockheed and Northrop are all located in the Los Angeles area.

In the post-war period California continued to prosper. Agriculture grew up into agribusiness; the film industry expanded into the new field of television; the aircraft industry was boosted by the space programme; and semiconductor technology paved the way for Silicon Valley.

Beatniks, Hippies and Modern Times

True to the tradition of California's indulgence of Utopian dreams, the Beat generation of the 1950s made its home in San Francisco's North Beach district. Writers such as Jack Kerouac and Allen Ginsberg, as well as the poets that hung round Lawrence Ferlinghetti's City Lights Bookstore, advocated a free and unstructured style of writing, exemplified by Jack Kerouac's cult novel *On the Road*.

Ten years on, the term 'hippies' was coined for the flower children who gathered around the Haight-Ashbury district of San Francisco. These inhabitants of what Joan Didion was to call 'America's first teenage slum' dispensed a vision of love, peace and light, heavily laced with marijuana and more

dangerous types of drug such as LSD. The sixties also produced a distinctive Californian brand of rock music, with bands such as the Grateful Dead and Jefferson Airplane, and the legendary voice of Janis Joplin.

California was also in the forefront of student radicalism, beginning with the Free Speech Movement at Berkeley in 1964, and ending with the violent clashes at San Francisco State College in 1968 and the 1969 Berkeley demonstration in favour of a 'People's Park', when protestors were sprayed with teargas.

Black radicalism accelerated after the Watts riots in Los Angeles in 1965 and reached its peak with the Black Panthers in Oakland, a paramilitary organization led by Huey Newton, Eldridge Cleaver and Bobby Seale. The Watts riots were sinisterly echoed in the Los Angeles riots of 1992, when the same area of South-Central LA was ravaged by violence in response to video film of white police officers beating a black resident. **21**

America's continuous social revolution has always had a prominent place in Californian life. Pressures for some kind of change have been alternately encouraged and resisted as the state's volatile political establishment has swung back and forth between conserva-

Hollywood still draws many hopefuls coming to California in search of fame and fortune.

tives and progressives. Ronald Reagan, Republican and former Hollywood actor, served as Governor of California between 1966 and 1974 and as President of the United States from 1980-8. He was succeeded as Governor of California by Jerry Brown, known to many as 'Governor Moonbeam'. A left-wing Democrat who espoused Zen Bhuddism and the legalization of marijuana, he also imposed environmental protection measures and energy resources long before others began to see the wisdom of such policies.

The Loma Prieta earthquake of 17 October 1989 resulted in 67 deaths and billions of dollars' worth of damage in the San Francisco area. It served as a reminder that Californians continue to live in the shadow of The Big One – the major earthquake that experts predict will strike in the next 30 years. It says a lot for the attractions of Californian life – and the optimism of those who enjoy it – that despite this, millions still seek their future in the Golden State's promised land.

Where to Go

Many Californians would like to divide their state into two new states, North and South California – corresponding to what they believe to be two distinct frames of mind represented by San Francisco and Los Angeles. In fact you will find a little bit of both – San Francisco's sophistication and Los Angeles' sunny craziness – all over the place.

Our journey begins with San Francisco and its nearby attractions and works its way down the coast to Los Angeles and San Diego before heading inland to the mountains and deserts of the Sierra Nevada and Death Valley. You can turn this itinerary upside down if you prefer, but either way, you should also consider making an excursion to Las Vegas, California's favourite out-of-state playground.

You can get to almost all these places by train or bus, and air travel is quite cheap. However, the car is king, and it's difficult to enjoy the full scope of this vast and varied landscape without driving. San Francisco is unusual for California in that it is a walker's town, with buses and cable-cars to help you up and down the hills. Los Angeles is undeniably car country, though it is trying to alleviate its congestion and pollution by building a light-rail network. Out-of-town attractions such as the national parks, and especially Death Valley, are most easily reached by car, although once there it's more rewarding to leave your vehicle behind and explore on foot.

San Francisco

San Franciscans are quite unashamedly in love with their town. All over the city you see the boast, 'Everybody's Favorite City'. The town's natural setting, nestling in the hills around the bay, makes it uncommonly cosy; the zip in the air is invigorating, and even the fog that rolls in off the ocean seems more romantic than chilling.

23

If you have a car, one way to begin your visit is to take the **49-Mile Drive**, a comprehensive tour of the main sights, marked by blue signposts with a white seagull. This will help you get your bearings before you start to explore in detail. Stop off at **Twin Peaks**, south of Golden Gate Park, for an excellent panoramic view of the city and the bay.

Then park the car, put on a pair of comfortable walking shoes, and take to the city's first-class public transport system (see p.136). Start at the bridge. The city has more than one, but *the* one is, of course, the **Golden Gate Bridge**. The name Golden Gate was given to the city's harbour entrance in 1846 by Captain John Frémont, but the mile-wide channel lay unspanned until the bridge was completed in 1937, a masterpiece of engineering by Joseph Strauss. At 4,200ft (1,280m), it was the world's longest single span until surpassed by New York's Verrazano Narrows Bridge built in 1964, but few would deny that it remains the most beautiful suspension bridge in the world. It took four years to build and now takes four years to repaint – a job that begins again as soon as it's finished.

*S*an Francisco's magnificent waterfront setting earned it the nickname 'City by the Bay'.

Take a bus to the bridge entrance and then walk across – as exciting an urban adventure as climbing up the Eiffel Tower or the Empire State Building. The bridge trembles below your feet and the lampposts rattle as the wind whistles through swooping cables. But don't worry – the 746ft (227m) high towers are well

embedded in earthquake-proof foundations.

Visible in the distance is the **San Francisco–Oakland Bay Bridge**, known locally as just the Bay Bridge. This silver-grey structure swings across to Oakland via two suspension spans, a cantilever span, and a tunnel through Yerba Buena Island. It's the bridge you'll take to go to Berkeley (see p.39), and beyond there to the Californian Wine Country (see p.40).

Beneath the south end of the Golden Gate is **Fort Point National Historic Site**, the site of the brick fort built in 1861 to protect the entrance to the harbour. Guides in period dress conduct tours of the old defences. The fort lies within the grounds of the Presidio, headquarters of the US Sixth Army.

On your way to the yacht harbour you'll pass the **Palace of Fine Arts**, a restored relic of the Panama–Pacific International Exposition. Its Greco-Romanesque rotunda contrasts with the modern technological wizardry in the **Exploratorium** – a hands-on exhibi-

tion of lasers, computers and solar-operated musical instruments which is great fun for children on a rainy day.

The great age of sail, in which San Francisco played a major part, is commemorated in the yacht harbour by the majestic lines of the square-rigged ship, the SV *Balclutha,* and the other exhibits of the **National Maritime Museum**. The museum can be reached from downtown via the Powell-Hyde cable-car line.

The other main cable-car route, the Powell-Mason line, terminates at one of San Francisco's most popular sights – **Fisherman's Wharf**. Geared more today to tourists than fishing, the area offers dozens of seafood restaurants, as well as a good wax museum and the Guinness Museum of World Records. Seafood stands line the wharfside – though the fish is very likely to be imported – and there are two shopping centres, **Ghirardelli Square**, a converted red-brick former chocolate factory (there are good free concerts here at the weekend), and **The Cannery**, once a fruit-processing plant. The ferry to Alcatraz leaves from Pier 41 at the east end of the wharf.

ALCATRAZ

Of the many cruises you can take on San Francisco Bay, the most entertaining is a trip to the abandoned prison island of Alcatraz. The United States Rangers offer informative and witty self-guided audio tours around the former home of Al Capone as well as other convicts such as Robert Stroud, the famous 'Birdman of Alcatraz'. The name is a distortion of the Spanish Isla de Alcatraces (Pelican Island).

A 12-acre (4.8ha) rock with no cultivable soil, all the earth and water for the shrubs and trees there had to be shipped in by the US Army, for whom it had been a 'disciplinary barracks' until 1934. Separated from mainland San Francisco by 1½ miles (2.4km) of treacherous, ice-cold water, haunted by sharks and dangerous currents, it was the ideal location for America's most notorious federal penitentiary. However, it proved enormously expensive to run, and was closed down in 1963.

You will see what 'maximum security, minimum privilege' meant for Alcatraz's 300 inmates, each one alone in a tiny cell, with three 20-minute

Escape from Alcatraz

Officially, nobody ever escaped from Alcatraz. In all, 39 prisoners attempted it: 27 were caught, 7 were killed and 5 have never been found but are assumed drowned.

In 1962, at the very end of the island's grim history, John Paul Scott made it to the San Francisco shore by greasing his body to help withstand the cold. A party of students found him clinging to the rocks at Fort Point, just below the Golden Gate Bridge, completely exhausted. Not knowing he was an escaped prisoner they helpfully called the police to rescue the poor fellow in his hour of need.

recreation periods each day. There were 'luxuries' – hot showers so that inmates would be unable to acclimatize themselves to cold water and survive the chilly waters of San Francisco Bay; as well as remarkably good food. One inmate returning for the guided tour – surprisingly, some do, out of nostalgia – said the food was better than he had eaten in many San Francisco hotels. The prisoners named the cell rows after elegant streets of America such as New York's Park Avenue, LA's Sunset Boulevard and Michigan Avenue in Chicago. The gangster Al Capone's cell was on 'B' Block, 2nd tier, No. 200.

THE HILLS

There are around 40 of them, and they're steep – it's been said that if you get tired walking around San Francisco you can just lean against it – but you don't have to tackle them all on foot. A tour of Nob Hill (from California Street or by Powell-Hyde cable-car), Telegraph Hill (bus) and Russian Hill (Powell-Hyde cable-car) will give you a good sense of the past and present splendours of San Francisco's more wealthy residents.

The cable-cars were installed in 1873 by Scottish engineer Andrew Hallidie, and one of the originals can still be seen in the fascinating **Cable Car Barn and Museum** at Washington and Mason, which is also the system's working powerhouse. The hand-made cars are the city's best-loved attraction, and the system was

Colourful Victorian houses line a quiet square on the edge of the city.

28

declared a National Historic Landmark in 1964.

The monumental Victorian houses of **Nob Hill** – home of the 'nobs' (possibly a derivation of 'nabobs') – were wiped out in the 1906 earthquake, and only the imposing brownstone house of James Flood, now the very exclusive Pacific Union Club, survived. Sadly, you won't be able to get in, but you can loiter (with appropriate decorum) in the area's two landmark hotels, the Fairmont and the Mark Hopkins. The panoramic view from the bars in the Crown Room or the Top of the Mark is well worth the stiff price of a drink.

Grace Cathedral, at the corner of California and Jones, is not an especially happy neo-Gothic effort, but it is worth a look in passing for its Ghiberti doors – bronze reproductions of the Baptistery East Doors in Florence – a remarkable example of San Francisco's continuing romance with Europe. You may also be impressed by the 12 stained-glass windows dedicated to 'Human Endeavor' depicting, among others,

Albert Einstein, Frank Lloyd Wright, Franklin D Roosevelt and Henry Ford.

Russian Hill is less opulent than Nob Hill, but the gardens

The famous cable-cars clank noisily up and down the steep hills of San Francisco. **29**

and immaculate little cottages of this fashionable residential area make it far more appealing. The roller-coaster dips and crests of the city's hills, breaking up the monotony of the standard grid system of streets, reach a crazy climax on **Lombard Street** between Hyde and Leavenworth. After you've negotiated all seven hairpin bends lined with gardens of hydrangeas, you're not going to quibble about the claim that it's the '**crookedest street in the world**'. Two blocks south is Filbert Street boasting the steepest slope – a stomach-churning 31.5 percent gradient, with no bends.

It is worth climbing to the top of **Telegraph Hill** for the view of the bay from the top of Coit Tower, built in 1934 to honour the city's fire department. One of San Francisco's many landmarks, its shape is meant to resemble the nozzle of a fire hose. Inside you will find Social Realist murals depicting 'Life in California, 1934'. Take a look at the cottages and gardens around the Greenwich Steps, clinging to

the steep slope overlooking the bay – one of the city's most desirable addresses.

DOWNTOWN

Market Street forms the main axis of San Francisco's city centre, and halfway along at the Powell Street cable-car terminus, is the San Francisco Visitors Information Center (see p.140), where you can pick up a free map before you set off to explore the surrounding area.

A few blocks along Powell Street is **Union Square**, the heart of downtown's shopping and theatre district. Here you can browse in speciality shops, fashionable boutiques and department stores such as the famous Macy's.

Head down to Montgomery Street, the heart of San Francisco's financial district, also known as the 'Wall Street of the West'. This was founded on the profits of the 1849 Gold Rush (see p.14), and is now bristling with skyscrapers of chrome and glass. Take a look at the Old Coin and Gold Exhibit at the **Bank of California** (400 California St), with its collection of gold coins and currency, or the **Wells Fargo History Room** in the Wells Fargo Bank (420 Montgomery St), which displays Gold Rush memorabilia, including one of the original Wells Fargo stage coaches. You're not likely to miss the **Transamerica Pyramid**, an 853ft (256m) spike at the corner of Montgomery and Washington. It's one of those buildings that purists start off hating because it clashes with the 'spirit' of San Francisco, and then defend in the next generation as the very epitome of its age.

Walk the few blocks uphill to Grant Street and suddenly you're in **Chinatown**. This compact district has evolved from a ghetto (imposed on the Chinese in the 19th century by the city's founders) into a proud, self-assertive community that has won the city's admiration. There are more than 82,000 Chinese living in the city, making it the largest Chinese community outside of Asia. Chinatown is bounded by Broadway, Bush, Kearny and Stockton, with the eight blocks along Grant Avenue making up its colourful centre.

At the Bush Street end of Grant Avenue, you will enter Chinatown through the ornamental **Chinatown Gateway**. The shops, the restaurants and street signs all have an English

Towering above other buildings on the streets of North Beach is the Transamerica Pyramid.

*D*elicate oriental tiles mark the Chinatown Gateway, entrance to San Francisco's lively Chinatown.

translation beside the Chinese characters for the benefit of tourists, but the banks, travel agencies and law offices don't always make the same concession. Not that you won't see the influence of American culture in institutions such as the **32** Catholic St Mary's Chinese School at Clay and Stockton, or in the neo-Gothic Old St Mary's Church.

Portsmouth Square, situated between Clay and Washington streets, was the city's original town square, where Sam Brannan announced the discovery of gold in 1848 (see p.14). But what really grabs your attention is the chatter of Chinese voices, the crowds, the colour, the smells of five-spice and dried shrimp – it's a little corner of Hong Kong right in the middle of California.

At Columbus Avenue, Chinatown spills over into **North Beach**, a Little Italy of cafés, bakeries, restaurants, grocery stores and ice-cream parlours. This lively neighbourhood is both the centre of the Italian community and the focus of the city's intellectual and artistic life. From the days when the poet Lawrence Ferlinghetti gathered fellow Beats around his City Lights Bookstore during the 1950s, North Beach has been a hangout for the bohemian literary crowd. City Lights, which opened in 1953, was America's first paperback bookshop, and is still going strong today, open daily until midnight.

Once you've bought your copy of *On the Road*, cross Jack Kerouac Street and settle down with your purchase over a drink at Vesuvio's, another famous literary hangout. Or if it's a sunny day, buy a sandwich from the delicatessen and enjoy a picnic on Washington Square, a splash of green overlooked by the white spires of the Church of SS Peter and Paul, where Marilyn Monroe and Joe DiMaggio were married in 1954.

The area around the south end of Columbus Avenue was once known as the Barbary Coast, a seedy and boisterous waterfront district, with sailors on shore leave haunting the bars and brothels, while their captains shanghaied drunken civilians to make up lost crew. The Barbary Coast was burned down after the Great Earthquake of 1906, but its tawdry tradition lives on in the now ever dwindling number of topless bars and strip clubs along Broadway.

Rather more highbrow entertainment is on offer in the angle between Market Street and Van Ness Avenue, where there is a sprawling complex of municipal, state and federal buildings known collectively as the **Civic Center**. It was initiated during a burst of city planning after the 1906 earthquake, and the early structures – note especially the green-domed City Hall and the handsome Public Library – form the finest grouping of French Renaissance architecture in **33** the country. Opposite the City Hall are the twin façades of the Veterans' Building (which houses the San Francisco Museum of Modern Art), and the War Memorial Opera House, where, in 1945, the United Nations Charter was signed; plus the curved glass front of the Louise M Davies Symphony Hall, home of the San Francisco Symphony Orchestra.

The district to the south of Market Street was once an area of slums, warehouses and railroad yards, but redevelopment combined with low rents have attracted a new interest. **SoMa**, as it is known (short for south of Market), is now home to the huge Moscone Convention Center, and the surrounding streets have become the focus of the city's trendiest nightlife, with dozens of new restaurants and nightclubs.

GOLDEN GATE PARK

Escape from the downtown skyscrapers by taking the No. 5 Fulton Street bus to Golden Gate Park. The park was once **34** a wasteland of sand dunes and

scrub, but it was then transformed into lush parkland by the efforts of John McLaren, the park superintendent for 50 years until his death in 1943.

Today the park is a delightful landscape of woods, rhododendron groves, small lakes and hills, with an arboretum, botanic gardens, sports fields, bicycle routes, riding stables and a popular open-air chess court known as the Card Shelter. At the eastern end there's a wonderful children's playground, and the lovely Conservatory of Flowers, a Victorian glasshouse from Britain.

Beyond the park lies the **Haight-Ashbury district**, famous as the scene of the sixties' 'Summer of Love', when thousands of flower children flocked into the city. Today you are more likely to spot yuppies than hippies, as an infusion of brand new shops as well as fashionable boutiques, along with some steady gentrification, promises continuous improvement.

Situated within the park are three major museums clustered around the Music Con-

City Hall provides a focus for the grand architectural ensemble of Civic Center.

course. The **M H de Young Memorial Museum** has an impressive selection of works by Titian, El Greco and Rembrandt. However, it is better known for its outstanding collection of North American art from 1670 to the 20th century.

The **Asian Art Museum** next door exhibits over 10,000 magnificent treasures of Oriental art, donated to San Francisco in 1966 by the Chicago millionaire Avery Brundage. Across the way you will find the **California Academy of Sciences**, housing an excellent natural history museum, an aquarium and a planetarium (opening after renovation in spring 1994).

The western end of the park boasts two turn-of-the-century windmills which overlook the surf at **Ocean Beach**. Chilly water and dangerous currents make this more a beach for strollers, sunbathers and experienced surfers – swimming is **35** not a good idea. The northern end of the beach is overlooked by the Cliff House, which was built in 1909 and now houses a restaurant and museum. There is also a fine view of the Seal Rocks, a favourite haunt of sealions and, on a clear day, the Farallon Islands 30 miles (48km) offshore.

Roller skaters slalom their way through the greenery of Golden Gate Park.

The Bay Area and Beyond

The City of San Francisco covers only 46 sq miles (119sq km) at the tip of its peninsula, but its suburbs and satellite communities, with a population of 6 million, spread all around the bay.

The Bay Area (as it is known) includes The Peninsula to the south, with the cities of Palo Alto and San Jose, and the computer industry heartland of Silicon Valley; the East Bay, across the Bay Bridge, which includes Oakland and the university town of Berkeley; and Marin County, San Francisco's most wealthy and desirable suburb, with its hills, forests and pretty villages. Further north lie the wine-growing regions of the Napa and Sonoma valleys.

MARIN COUNTY

Immediately north of San Francisco are two charming waterfront towns – **Sausalito** and **Tiburon**, which you can reach either by driving across the Golden Gate Bridge or by taking a ferry – from the Ferry Building at the foot of Market Street for Sausalito, or Pier 43½ near Fisherman's Wharf for Tiburon.

Tiburon is the quieter of the two, while Sausalito is more of a tourist trap, but both have a colourful Mediterranean atmosphere, with art galleries, yacht harbours, craft shops, and pleasant bistros and cafés out on the boardwalk overlooking the bay.

Further inland is the lovely town of Mill Valley, and behind it rises the 2,604ft (794m) summit of **Mount Tamalpais**.

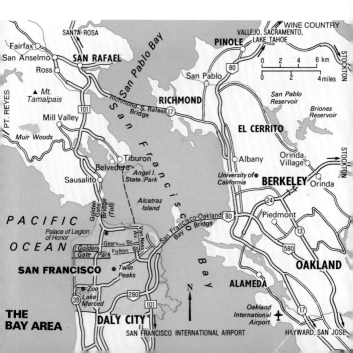

The mountain bike was invented here in the 1970s and there are plenty of hiking and biking trails – but if you're feeling lazy you can drive along the Panoramic Highway to within a few hundred yards of the summit. The view from the top is tremendous – across the bay to the city and then beyond to Mount Diablo, and on a clear day you might even catch a glimpse of the beautiful Sierra Nevada mountains.

Highway 1 twists through the hills to the coast, past the **Muir Woods National Monument**, named after John Muir,

The lucky residents of Sausalito houseboats relax in a quiet backwater of the bay.

the Scots-born environmentalist, who founded California's conservation movement at the turn of the 20th century. The park protects several groves of magnificent coastal redwoods, some of which are 250ft (76m) tall and over 1,000 years old. Hiking trails wind among the giant trees.

The highway continues on to **Point Reyes National Seashore**, a large wilderness park on the coast, complete with beautiful rolling hills, sandy bays and exciting wild surf. There, explore the bird-haunted lagoon at Drake's Bay, a peaceful cove where Francis Drake claimed California for England in 1579, or hike your way through the Earthquake Trail, a path which follows the trace of the San Andreas Fault.

BERKELEY

Take the BART subway from Market Street or drive across the Bay Bridge to make a pilgrimage to the **University of California** campus at Berkeley, the scene of the 1960's student radicalism. Opened in

---

Waiting for the Big One

San Francisco sits right on top of the San Andreas Fault, a major fracture in the earth's crust that runs north–west from the Gulf of California for 600 miles (965km), passing beneath the city and separating Point Reyes from the mainland. The BART subway tunnel between San Francisco and Oakland was bored right through the fault.

The Baja California peninsula and the coast to the west of the fault is moving north relative to the rest of North America, at an average of half an inch (1cm) a year. There has been no movement along the San Francisco section of the fault since the disastrous earthquake of 1906, but experts predict that there's a 50/50 chance of another major quake – the dreaded Big One – occurring in the next 30 years.

1873, this is the oldest of the University of California's nine campuses. Tours of the museums, library, gardens and other sights are organized from the Student Union at the end of Telegraph Avenue (Monday to Friday at 1pm). The free and easy access to the university's facilities will give you an insight into Berkeley's open personality. The nearby streets are lined with lively cafés and interesting bookshops.

WINE COUNTRY

The scenic valleys of Napa and Sonoma have been producing wine on a commercial basis since the middle of the 19th century, and today Californian

California's vineyards are justly famous as producers of some of the world's finest wines.

wines are considered to be among the finest in the world. There are more than 200 vineyards – or wineries as they are called – and most of them offer guided tours and tastings in the cellars. Some of the more interesting wineries to visit are Mondavi, Beringer, Martini and Beaulieu in Napa, and Souverain and Sebastiani in Sonoma.

You can drive to the vineyards from San Francisco via Interstate 80, across the Bay Bridge, but bus tours are also available. It's a good idea to contact an agency specializing in wine tours – the San Francisco Visitor Information Center (see p.140) can provide details. Harvests begin around mid-August – the Californian climate is so much more predictably sunny than Europe's.

A note of warning: the entire region, but in particular the Napa Valley, is inundated with visitors all year round, and you would be well advised to book ahead. Also, following the French tradition, the best restaurants of the region are closed on Tuesday.

The Central Coast

Highway 1 runs for 400 miles (643km) from San Francisco to LA, along a coastline of often quite spectacular beauty.

First stop for most tourists is the Monterey Peninsula, a wave-battered coast of gnarled cypress trees and jagged rocks, and the home of sealions, pelicans and otters. The principal town here is **Monterey**, the old Spanish and Mexican capital of Alta (Upper) California. Monterey Bay was discovered in 1542, but it wasn't settled until much later when Father Junípero Serra set up a mission in 1770. Serra's statue looks down on the bay from Corporal Ewin Road.

The town is proud of its past and offers a self-guided tour of all the Old Town's historic 19th-century buildings. Look out for the **Larkin House**, at Jefferson and Calle Principal, home of the first (and only) US Consul in the 1840s, as well as the **Stevenson House**, 530 Houston Street, where the Scottish writer Robert Louis **41**

Stevenson lived for 4 months after his arrival in California in 1879. Some think that the nearby coastline around Point Lobos provided the inspiration for the setting of his famous story, *Treasure Island.*

On Church Street you'll find the site of Father Serra's original adobe church. Rebuilt in 1795, it is now the **Royal Presidio Chapel** (or Cathedral of San Carlos de Borromeo). By the waterfront is the **Custom House Plaza**, with the new Maritime Museum as well as the Old Custom House (1827), where the American flag was raised by Commodore John Sloat in 1846 when he claimed Monterey for the USA.

Beside the Plaza is Monterey's **Fisherman's Wharf**. Like San Francisco's, it is a collection of souvenir shops and restaurants on the dock, offering a great view across the boats in the marina. The fish on sale is most definitely fresh, but alas, no longer abundant enough to keep Cannery Row going as more than a weatherbeaten curiosity. The famous sardine fisheries final-

ly closed down in the 1940s as a result of over-fishing, but the waterfront district of timbered canneries, immortalized by the novelist John Steinbeck as 'a poem, a stink, a grating noise, a quality of light, a tone, a habit, a nostalgia', has found a new lease of life today as a tourist attraction with souvenir shops, delightful cosy boutiques and artists' studios.

One old cannery building has been splendidly converted to the **Monterey Bay Aquarium**, one of the best aquariums in the world as well as being an educational showcase for the unique underwater environment of Monterey Bay. The centrepiece is the stunning 30ft (10m) Kelp Forest Tank, a window on California's most important marine habitat. Kids will love the Sea Otter Pool and the Touch Pools, where they can both handle and learn about sea anemones, crabs and even bat rays.

The 17-Mile Drive is a lovely scenic toll road starting at Lighthouse Avenue in **Pacific Grove**, a pleasant waterside town of Victorian houses and clapboard cottages a few miles beyond Monterey. The drive passes through beautiful cypress groves along a wild and rocky coastline, where you can watch birds, otters and sealions in the wild, before passing through the famous golf courses at Pebble Beach and finally reaching the exclusive resort town of **Carmel-by-the-Sea**, famous for once having Clint Eastwood as mayor. It is a quaint, picture-postcard village full of kitschy cottages, with narrow, tree-lined streets crammed with expensive restaurants, art galleries and craft shops. At the foot of Ocean Avenue lies the beautiful white sand of Carmel Beach, backed by shady pines and cypress

Historic Monterey was once the capital of Spanish California – the state constitution was drawn up here in 1850.

trees. South east of the town is the peaceful **Carmel Mission**, where Father Junípero Serra himself lies buried.

At **Point Lobos State Reserve** you can hike right down to the ocean's edge. Look out especially for the playful sea otters, which can often be seen floating on their backs munching on a juicy abalone or two and, from December to March, look out also for pods of migrating grey whales.

The coastal highway from Carmel to **Big Sur** is only 30 miles (48km) long, but it takes more than an hour of careful driving. Squeezed in between the Pacific and the Santa Lucia mountains, the road twists and turns along a quite narrow ledge hacked out high above the pounding surf, with spectacular bridges spanning the deep canyons.

The numerous state parks along the Big Sur coast offer marvellous opportunities for outdoor activities like camping, hiking and fishing. The writer Henry Miller made his home here during the 1950s and 60s, and communities of artists continue to live in cabins in the woods and canyons.

At Nepenthe, Orson Welles built a honeymoon cottage for Rita Hayworth in the days when film stars did the romantic things expected of them by their adoring public. Now it's been expanded and converted into a restaurant, well worth a

Peaceful Carmel Mission marks the beginning of the spectacular Big Sur coast.

visit for its incomparable view of the ocean.

The rugged coast continues for another 65 miles (105km) along to San Simeon, where William Randolph Hearst, the newspaper magnate immortalized by Orson Welles in the film *Citizen Kane*, built his unbelievable dream castle on a hilltop high above the sea. **Hearst Castle** now forms the centrepiece of the Hearst San Simeon State Historical Monument, and is second only to Disneyland as the most popular attraction in all California (guided tours only). Allow at least 2 hours for a tour – you can book one at the Visitor Center, but it's advisable to make an advance reservation, especially during the summer, by phoning 1 800 444 7275.

William Randolph Hearst (1863-1951) was a millionaire newspaper baron. He began building this grandiose retreat in 1919 on a ranch that he had inherited from his father,

who made his fortune mining Nevada's Comstock Lode. It was still not completed by the time of Hearst's death in 1951. Here he entertained the movie star Marion Davies, his mistress for 30 years, and famous guests such as Charlie Chaplin, Scott and Zelda Fitzgerald, Greta Garbo, Winston Churchhill, Charles Lindbergh and the photographer Herman Mankiewicz, who recorded life at San Simeon for posterity.

You approach Hearst Castle on a tour bus which climbs the 5 miles (8km) from the Visitor Center to the hilltop, passing through the parkland that was once Hearst's private zoo – the lions, monkeys, cheetahs, kangaroos and polar bears are long gone, but zebra, goats and Barbary sheep can still be seen grazing on the slopes.

The San Francisco architect Julia Morgan built the 'castle' to Hearst's specifications as a showcase for his extraordinary collection of European art. The truly mind-boggling variety of that collection begins to register as you pass the 104ft (32m) Roman mosaic swimming pool which is complete with Greek colonnade and a copy of Donatello's Florentine statue of David.

The main building and its four surrounding guest houses, with their terraces and gardens, is a fantasy concoction derived from Greek, Roman, Gothic, baroque and Spanish styles, with both fake and original artwork thrown together. Genuine Spanish tilework sits beside locally made copies; a Roman sarcophagus and a 3,500-year-old Egyptian goddess are both authentic, but the castle's façade, with its equestrian friezes on the balcony and Gothic-style canopies, is made almost completely of reinforced concrete. Above the huge main door, in quiet simplicity, sits a genuine 13th-century Madonna and Child.

Inside the castle, the hotchpotch of periods and styles runs riot. The dining room has

The rich and famous once partied by the luxurious Roman pool at Hearst Castle.

46

a magnificent cedarwood coffered ceiling from a Bologna monastery, and is decorated with the flags from the Sienna *palio* pageant. At the table set for 22 guests, Hearst's dilettantism is emphasized by the sight of splendid, solid silver Queen Anne candlesticks and wine cisterns, which are set beside tomato ketchup, pickles and mustard, all in their original bottles and jars.

Beyond San Simeon the coastline begins to relent, and

farms and oil rigs take the place of crags and canyons. Rural Route 1 joins the multilane Federal Highway 101 at San Luis Obispo for the final leg to Los Angeles, but two places are worth a detour from the freeway.

The city of **Lompoc** (Route 135 and Route 1 from Santa Maria) sits very prettily among the fields of flowers that have made it the 'Flower-Growing Capital of the World'. On the edge of town is **La Purisima Mission**, founded in 1787 and rebuilt in 1813 after an earthquake. It is the most extensively and authentically restored of California's 21 Franciscan missions, and the old pink and white adobe walls provide a haven of peace amid the old living and working quarters of missionaries, soldiers and Indians. The garden is full of olive and mulberry trees, and livestock such as *burros* (don-

Mission Santa Barbara basks contentedly in the southern Californian sunshine.

keys), turkeys and four-horned *churro* sheep, all contribute to the 1820s atmosphere.

When you get to **Santa Barbara** you know for sure that you've arrived in southern California. Its palm-fringed streets, red-tile pavements and low-rise Spanish Revival buildings spread up the hillsides from the beautiful beach, oozing sun-tanned health and the scent of money. It's a favourite weekend retreat for Los Angeles' wealthier residents, and home to the likes of ex-president Ronald Reagan and pop star Michael Jackson.

There's history on display, too: at the museum in the Santa Barbara Presidio State Historic Park, in the town centre, and at the **Mission Santa Barbara**, which lies further up the hill. The mission, which was founded on 4 December 1786, the Feast of St Barbara, offers a self-guided tour of its restored church and outbuildings. Also worth a visit is the beautifully styled Santa Barbara County Courthouse – a magnificent Spanish-Moorish edifice dating from 1927.

Los Angeles

Los Angeles is the quintessential 20th-century city. Only modern technology could have turned this former patch of desert into one of the world's most flourishing metropolises.

A combination of engineering genius and shady business deals brought water hundreds of miles across mountains and desert to slake the city's thirst and nurture its lush gardens and palm trees. An abundance of space then allowed the city to sprawl, but distance was no problem – cheap oil and the car produced a vast freeway system, which links the coast, the hills and the farthest-flung valleys in one huge conurbation. Visitors flying into LA at night get a grand view of the network of traffic arteries, with cars and trucks surging along like blood corpuscles pumping through the veins of some living organism.

LA covers such an immense area that the first-time visitor can easily feel overwhelmed. The best way to approach the **49** city is to break it down into smaller regions and then take them one at a time – Downtown, Hollywood, Westside, The Coast, The Valleys and Orange County.

DOWNTOWN

LA's downtown commercial district is steadily becoming a more attractive and culturally active area, and is developing into something of a focal point for the city. It lies at the hub of the freeway system, and of the planned light-rail network, the Metro. Historically, too, this is the heart of Los Angeles. **El Pueblo de Los Angeles State Historic Park** preserves a few blocks of the original Mexican village around which the city grew up. The centrepiece is Olvera Street, a bustling Mexican marketplace lined with colourful stalls and historic buildings, including the Avila Adobe, which dates from 1818 and is LA's oldest surviving building. Half of California's Mexican-American (*chicano*) population lives in central Los Angeles, and the lively Mexi-

can atmosphere is best enjoyed at Grand Central Market, north of Pershing Square.

Just north of the Pueblo are the crowded streets and Oriental architecture of LA's **Chinatown**, while to the south is **Little Tokyo**, the centre of the Japanese community. The Japanese Village Mall is a popular shopping spot, with twisting paths lined with bonsai trees, rock gardens and sushi bars. Nearby is a monument to the Space Shuttle *Challenger*, including a statue of the Japan-

---

CAR CULTURE

Greater Los Angeles has been designed around the automobile – there are 1,500 miles (2,413km) of freeways, and 25 percent of the urban land area is occupied by car parks.

In fact, if you want to, you can order a burger, pay a cheque into your bank, watch a movie, listen to a church sermon and even return your library books all without leaving the driver's seat.

ese-American astronaut Ellison Onizuka, one of the seven who died in the 1986 disaster.

The most dynamic area of downtown is the commercial district around Flower Street. Many of the new cultural institutions that have surfaced in recent years are here. The beautiful **Museum of Contemporary Art (MOCA)** at California Plaza is a striking setting for important works by Mondrian, Robert Rauschenberg and Jackson Pollock, as well as many other innovative American artists. MOCA curators keep one step ahead of the pack by commissioning new work, which is then displayed beside contemporary classics. The **Temporary Contemporary** gallery in Central Avenue is an annex to MOCA, and houses travelling exhibitions.

The **Music Center**, at First Street and Grand, is an important LA venue for concerts and plays, which are performed in the Dorothy Chandler Pavilion, the Mark Taper Forum and the Ahmanson Theater. There are tours of the Center's architecture and sculpture.

A few miles south west of central downtown, next to the University of Southern California campus, lies **Exposition Park**, the setting for the 1932 Olympics. Among the sports stadia you can also explore half a dozen excellent museums, and wander through the

Traffic surges relentlessly along the immense, ten-lane freeways of downtown Los Angeles.

*E*xotic fruits from nearby islands in the South Pacific fill the stalls at LA's 'Farmers' Market'.

Rose Garden, whose 16,000 rose bushes are at their most splendid in springtime.

Further south still is the district of Watts. Besides being notorious as the black neighbourhood that erupted in violent anger in 1965 and 1992, the district boasts one of the city's more bizarre and exhilarating monuments, the **Watts Towers**, at 1765 East 107th Street, off the Harbor Freeway. This was constructed between 1921 and 1954 by a tile-setter, Simon Rodia, out of old scrap steel and wire, and decorated with coloured pottery shards, sea shells, glass and pebbles cemented to the frames.

If you're heading west from downtown, avoid the freeway this time and follow another great thoroughfare, **Wilshire Boulevard**. Glittering with the prosperity of its department stores and luxury hotels, it is also a living museum of the art-deco architecture that characterized Los Angeles' rise to greatness during the twenties and thirties.

Notable buildings include the Bullocks Wilshire department store (now I Magnin's) at the corner of Kingsley, and the Franklin Life Insurance building situated at Van Ness and 5209 Wilshire.

*M*ann's Chinese Theater houses a cinema that's as big an attraction as the movie it shows.

Further west along Wilshire lies Hancock Park, which contains the famous **La Brea Tar Pits**. Here petroleum deposits ooze through fractures to the surface and evaporate, leaving natural tar lakes (*brea* is Spanish for 'tar'). The neighbouring **George C Page Museum** has on display the skeletons of mammoths, mastodons, sabre-toothed tigers and other unfortunate creatures who became trapped in the sticky tar during the last Ice Age.

Next door to the Tar Pits is the **Los Angeles County Museum of Art**, whose provocative modern architecture houses one of the state's best art collections, including outstanding examples of Nepalese and Indian and Tibetan art, Japanese scroll paintings, pre-Columbian art and German Expressionist drawings. Other highlights include important

works by Rembrandt, Dürer, Frans Hals, Picasso and the Impressionists.

HOLLYWOOD

The hand, foot and hoof prints of Hollywood stars have been immortalized in the concrete courtyard of **Mann's Chinese Theater** (at 6925 Hollywood Boulevard) in the heart of Tinseltown since 1927. Most stars were obliged to get on their knees and make a hand print, but it was natural for Fred Astaire to leave a footprint, John Wayne to leave a fist print, and cowboy Tom Mix to leave his horse's hoof print. Other rather unusual impressions on view **53** are Paul Newman's bare feet, Shirley Temple's toes, George Burns' cigar, Jimmy Durante's nose, and the tracks of R2D2 from *Star Wars*. See if your anatomy is the same size!

*C*elebrity feet, hands and noses grace the sidewalk outside Mann's Chinese Theater.

54

Take a walk along Hollywood Boulevard, one of the rare parts of LA where walking is customary, and you'll see over 2,500 actors' names on bronze stars embedded in the pavement – the **Walk of Fame**. You'll pass Frederic's of Hollywood with its lingerie museum, and the beautifully restored Roosevelt Hotel. Between La Brea and Western Avenue, the boulevard still exhibits the fine, tacky splendour of the 1920s and 30s, with its low, flat stucco buildings, a droopy palm tree or two, and even some vintage Packards and Buicks parked out on the street. The neighbourhood itself, however, is less than scintillating, although the second-hand bookstores specializing in film-related books and posters are excellent. The studios themselves have long since moved over the hills to set up shop in North Hollywood and Burbank.

A few blocks north of the boulevard is the **Hollywood Bowl**, the splendid open-air auditorium where the Los Angeles Philharmonic Orchestra holds concerts under the gigantic illuminated letters of the HOLLYWOOD sign planted up in the hills.

South of Hollywood Boulevard is LA's most famous street, **Sunset Boulevard**. The section between Hollywood and Beverly Hills is known simply as 'The Strip', and in the heyday of the thirties and forties this was a playground of the rich and famous, lined with the latest nightclubs and restaurants.

One of the most enjoyable Hollywood trips is a tour of the film and television studios. Two major TV networks – CBS and NBC – welcome you on to their sets for a look behind the scenes at some of America's most popular TV shows. A limited number of tickets to live shows are available. **Universal Studios**, just north of the Hollywood Freeway, offers an elaborate tour in open trolleys. In the course of displays of special-effects trickery you'll be caught in the crossfire of a space-age laser battle, attacked by the shark from *Jaws,* meet up with a three-storey-tall King Kong, and be subjected to all the earthquakes, floods and fires you ever saw in a disaster movie. You can also take a look behind the scenes and learn about techniques which are used to create film's great illusions. The highlight is the *Back To The Future* ride. Seated in a flight simulator shaped like the famous time-travelling DeLorean car in the films, you will be taken on a hair-raising chase through time and space, backwards to the Ice Age and forwards to the 21st century.

Warner Brothers and Columbia are located at Burbank Studios (just off the Ventura Freeway). They organize tours for smaller groups around the special effects and prop departments and the back-lots – even during the shooting of a film, if you're lucky.

While you're on the north side of town, take a drive around the Hollywood Hills for a superb view of the city. The classic Los Angeles cruise is along **Mulholland Drive**. On a clear day you can see Long Beach, 25 miles (40km) **55** away across the vast, sprawling metropolis.

Another great viewpoint is the Observatory in **Griffith Park**. The USA's biggest city park sprawls across the eastern Hollywood Hills and is crisscrossed with drives and hiking trails. Fans of James Dean will recognise the Observatory – it was the scene of the climax of *Rebel Without a Cause*. The panorama from the terrace on a clear day is fantastic, from the spiky skyscrapers of downtown to the distant Pacific. Towards sunset is the best time to go, just as the city lights are coming on.

WESTSIDE

The western edge of Hollywood merges with the slopes of Laurel Canyon and **Beverly Hills**, dotted with the sumptuous mansions of the movie moguls. While these homes are heavily guarded and hidden from view, you can sense the opulent atmosphere as you drive through the plush, carefully manicured avenues. The architecture is an astounding mixture of Spanish, Gothic, Bauhaus and Renaissance, in every pastel shade under the sun. Watch out for street vendors selling 'official' maps showing the homes of the rich and famous – they are probably bogus, and in any case, there's usually nothing to see except a security gate.

Beverly Hills is phenomenally clean and dropping litter is almost a capital crime. The area is policed with formidable efficiency and, except for the great shopping streets such as Rodeo Drive, anyone walking is viewed with some suspicion, especially at night. If you do want to take a walk here, put on tennis or sports clothes and the police will just assume you're a jogger.

There's a more scholarly feel to Los Angeles around the campus of UCLA (University of California – Los Angeles) at **Westwood Village** – but it's still a lot of fun. The Village, unlike neighbouring Beverly Hills, is a great place to stroll around the streets, and you can visit the best cinemas in town – new films always open here

Lofty, graceful palms line the broad, neat boulevards of affluent Beverly Hills.

first. If Hollywood has filled you with nostalgia for the great days of cinema, then you might like to pay homage to Marilyn Monroe in Westwood Memorial Park (1212 Glendon Ave, south of Wilshire Boulevard), where a modest plaque bears silent immortal testimony to the actress.

THE COAST

'The beach', as locals always refer to it, stretches some 40 miles (64km) from Malibu, through Santa Monica, Venice, Marina del Rey, Hermosa and Redondo to Palos Verdes, before the white sands run into the pollution around the San Pedro and Long Beach shipyards. There's no better way to get the special feel of Los Angeles than by heading right down to the beach. In LA the beach is not just for holidays and weekends – it's a year-round playground, community centre, gymnasium, solarium and singles bar.

Malibu is the favoured residence of the more relaxed members of Hollywood's film community. Rather than barricade themselves behind electrified fences guarded by huge Dobermans, as they do in Bel Air and Beverly Hills, film actors and hot young directors can be seen jogging along the seashore or simply gathering in their groceries at the local supermarket.

J ust one of the many varied and colourful characters who frequent the boardwalk at Venice Beach.

Perhaps the most famous attraction here is the **J Paul Getty Museum** at 17985 West Pacific Coast Highway, Malibu (phone ahead on 458 2003 for reserved parking in the museum garage, or take bus 434 from Santa Monica). At first the museum buildings

awaken echoes of Hearst Castle at San Simeon (see p.45). It is undoubtedly a serious art collection, but its setting – in a vast replica of a palatial Roman villa – has something of the pretentious inclinations of San Simeon, without Hearst's pick-and-mix flamboyance.

J P Getty had a more coherent idea of the kind of art he wanted to collect – Greek, Roman, Renaissance, baroque and French rococo. The collection of antiquities is impressive, highlighted by the 'Getty bronze', a 4th-century BC statue of an Olympic champion, believed by some experts to be the only remaining work of Lysippus, court sculptor of Alexander the Great. Among the paintings are superb works by Raphael, Rubens, van Dyck and Rembrandt.

Malibu's **Surfrider Beach** attracts surfers from all over the world as well as the locals, many riding the old-fashioned 'big guns' – boards at least 10ft (3m) long. Malibu Pier is a good place to fish, but sunbathing and swimming are a little more peaceful along the road at Las Tunas and Topanga beaches. The only natural hazard which can disturb Malibu's cheerful complacency is the odd storm tide or landslide which washes the precarious beach houses into the Pacific.

In contrast, **Santa Monica** is built on more solid ground, befitting the middle-class community that inhabits it. This attractive seaside town is one of the most pleasant places to stay in LA, and is very popular with people in the arts and the entertainment industries. At night there are many good restaurants, clubs and theatres to enjoy, and by day there is the glorious beach, complete

Surfers queue to catch the perfect right-hand break at Malibu's impressive Surfrider Beach.

Symbol of an era of style and elegance, the Queen Mary *dominates the Long Beach shoreline.*

Albert Kinney, planned construction of a replica of Venice here, but shortly after work started, oil was discovered and the idea was abandoned. The neighbourhood has now been revived as a diverse community of artists, writers and bohemian types. It is the Venice artists who have pioneered the street-painting that has spread throughout LA – the *trompe l'oeil* murals covering whole façades, often three or four storeys high, some creating optical illusions by depicting mirror images of the street on which they appear.

South of Marina del Rey, the world's largest small-boat harbour, the **beaches** continue in an unbroken golden curve – Dockweiler, Manhattan, Hermosa, Redondo – to the rocky bluffs of Palos Verdes. Around the point lies San Pedro, the Port of Los Angeles, and the city of Long Beach.

with an amusement pier, antique carousel and the nearby shopping arcades.

However, it is neighbouring **Venice** that attracts all the attention. The beach and boardwalk are a non-stop open-air circus of LA's extroverts and eccentrics, all vying with each other to be the centre of atten-**60** tion. In 1892 a millionaire,

Long Beach – which is 7 miles (11km) long, in fact – is the last resting place of one of the world's biggest ever cruise ships, the ***Queen Mary***, a nostalgic reminder of the grand era of luxury ocean liners. Since being moored here in 1969, the *Queen Mary*'s staterooms have been turned into a hotel, and her dining rooms into a restaurant; the rest of the ship is open to the public with self-guided tours (admission is free). Launched on the River Clyde in Scotland in 1934 for the Cunard line, the *Queen Mary* is 1,019ft (310m) long, displaces 81,237 tons, and carried a complement of 1,174 officers and crew, with accommodation for 1,959 passengers. Firework displays are staged over her on Friday and Saturday night during summer.

THE VALLEYS

The great mass of Los Angeles' population lives in the sprawling suburbs of the Valleys – the San Fernando Valley north of the Hollywood Hills and the San Gabriel Valley stretching east towards San Bernardino. There is very little here to interest the visitor, but there are two important art galleries situated in the lower San Gabriel Valley.

Pasadena is one of the oldest and richest Valley suburbs, home to the renowned California Institute of Technology (Caltech) and the handsome, modern **Norton Simon Museum** at Orange Grove and Colorado, just off the Ventura Freeway. This museum houses a truly remarkable range of

An impromptu roller dance performance entertains the crowd at Venice Beach.

European paintings, drawings and sculpture from the early Renaissance to the 20th century, along with Indian bronzes and Asian stone carvings. Outstanding attractions are works by Raphael, Botticelli, Rembrandt, Rubens and Cézanne. You will also find an extensive collection of drawings by Picasso and, one of the museum's great joys, the Degas bronzes. The sculpture garden includes works by Maillol, Picasso, Rodin, Giacometti and **62** Henry Moore.

The neighbouring suburb of San Marino was once owned by railroad tycoon Henry E Huntington (1850-1927), and his fine mansion now houses the **Huntington Library**. Its collection of rare books includes one of the First Folios of Shakespeare, a Gutenberg Bible and Benjamin Franklin's autobiography. The most seductive attraction is perhaps the **Botanical Gardens**.

Just 20 minutes' drive east from downtown LA is the recently opened **Cerritos Center for the Performing Arts**. Overnight and with just a few boxes, 10 people can turn an avant-garde theatre into a luxurious opera house or cabaret with a foyer in the tradition of the Paris Opéra. This technical wonder is part of the new town of **Cerritos**.

ORANGE COUNTY

Orange County, bedrock conservative southern California, is birthplace of disgraced ex-president Richard Nixon, land of the lawn sprinkler and two-car garage, and home to the legendary blue-rinsed little old ladies in tennis shoes. Along the coast, however, you can rediscover the beach culture that gave birth to the Beach Boys, and at Anaheim you can indulge yourself in the delights of California's number one tourist attraction.

Anaheim, 27 miles (43km) south-east of downtown LA on the Santa Ana freeway, is the home of **Disneyland**. It's best to allow a full day for a visit, as the entrance fee is expensive, and there is so much to see. You can buy a Passport for one, two or three days, covering the entire Disneyland complex and valid for unlimited use on all the attractions. Food and drink is extra.

*T*housands of children (not to mention their parents!) thrill daily to the delights of Walt Disney's magical world of Disneyland.

Main Street sets the tone with its sunny evocation of small-town USA at the turn of the century. The houses and shops are all three-quarter size – in his effort to escape from the realities of the outside world Disney made everything a little smaller than in real life.

Adventureland is a boat trip through simulated jungle on a river that makes its way successively through Asia, Africa and the South Pacific.

A miniature railroad carries you through Frontierland, the pioneer country of the Old West where loudspeakers warn you to 'watch out for Indians and wild animals'.

Tomorrowland is one of the most exciting theme parks and is constantly being renovated to keep pace with technological progress. The various rides include a submarine, a spaceship bound for Mars and up-to-date experiments in public transport. Two new attractions are Mickey's ToonTown, a 3-dimensional and living cartoon world, as well as Fantasmic!, an after-dark light and sound **64** spectacular where heroes and villains clash inside Mickey's imagination.

North-west of Disneyland you will find the **Movieland Wax Museum** (7711 Beach Boulevard, Buena Park) which displays wax figures of film stars in scenes from their best-known films. For film buffs, the most interesting display will be the collection of old nickelodeons, autoscopes and movieola machines that projected the very first moving pictures.

Just one block south of the Wax Museum yet another kind of fantasy can be experienced at **Knott's Berry Farm** where the American Wild West is brought to life in three different theme park areas. The Wild West Ghost Town, White Water Rapids Ride, loop-the-loop roller coaster, and the Good Time Theater will keep cowboy fans entertained for hours on end. Then if you feel a little peckish after all that action, you can feast on the boysenberry pies and chicken dinners with which Mrs Knott started up her business over 50 years ago.

A Selection
of Hotels and
Restaurants
in California

Recommended Hotels

California offers a wide range of accommodation in all price brackets, from basic motels and youth hostels to bed and breakfast inns and five-star luxury hotels. Reservations are strongly recommended – if you are calling from within the USA, use the toll-free 800 telephone numbers listed in the entries below. You may want to inquire about weekly rates, weekend discounts and family schemes (ie no charge for children occupying the same room as their parents).

Unless you are on a pre-paid tour, meals are not included in the price of a room. Almost all rooms have bathroom, air-conditioning and television, and many hotels and motels have swimming pools. Many places in Los Angeles, San Diego and San Francisco offer reduced rates and full-board arrangements from Friday to Sunday to offset the drop in business travel at the weekend. Reduced rates are also offered during the winter months. Visitors travelling by car should check whether an extra fee is charged for parking. Note that all room rates are subject to a 'transient occupancy' tax, currently 12.5 percent in Los Angeles and 11 percent in San Francisco.

As a basic guide, the symbols below indicate high-season rates for a double room with bath or shower. Breakfast is not normally included in the price:

▌	up to $75
▌▌	$75–125
▌▌▌	over $125

LOS ANGELES – DOWNTOWN

Best Western Mayfair Hotel ▌▌
1256 W. 7th Street, Los Angeles, CA 90017
Tel. (213) 484 9789; 800 821 868
Fax (213) 484 2769

Fine old hotel with an elegant art deco restaurant. Free parking for guests. 295 rooms.

Biltmore Hotel ▌▌▌
506 S. Grand Avenue, Los Angeles, CA 90071
Tel. (213) 624 1011; 800 245 8673
Fax (213) 612 1545

A grand old 1920s landmark now restored to its full former glory. Breathtakingly magnificent lobby, and gracious dining in Bernard's Restaurant or the Grand Avenue Bar. 700 rooms.

Figueroa Hotel ▮▮

939 S. Figueroa Street, Los Angeles, CA 90015
Tel. (213) 627 8971;
800 421 9092
Fax (213) 689 0305

A charming Spanish-style hotel with comfortable rooms, a palm-fringed courtyard, outdoor pool and spa bath. 285 rooms.

Motel de Ville ▮

1123 W. 7th Street, Los Angeles, CA 90017
Tel. (213) 624 8474
Fax (213) 624 7652

Good-value basic motel only a short walk from the centre of Los Angeles. Rooms have air-conditioning and satellite TV. Heated outdoor pool and coffee shop. 62 rooms.

New Otani Hotel and Garden ▮▮▮

120 S. Los Angeles Street, Los Angeles, CA 90012
Tel. (213) 629 1200;
800 273 2294
Fax (213) 622 0980

Attentive service and comfortable rooms decorated in restful shades of pink with a distinctive Japanese flavour. Ornamental Japanese garden, plus a choice of either American or Japanese restaurants. 455 rooms.

Westin Bonaventure Hotel ▮▮▮

404 S. Figueroa Street, Los Angeles, CA 90071
Tel. (213) 624 1000;
800 228 3000
Fax (213) 612 4894

From the outside it's a gleaming cluster of glass towers dominating the downtown skyline. Inside you will find a six-storey atrium complete with pond and fountains, lush hanging greenery, bar, restaurants and a shopping centre. Luxurious rooms with five-star service. Outdoor swimming pool. A vast 1,474 rooms.

Wilshire Royale Hotel ▮▮▮

2619 Wilshire Boulevard, Los Angeles, CA 90057
Tel. (213) 387 5311;
800 421 8072
Fax (213) 380 8174

Elegant art deco-style hotel with plush and spacious bedrooms and suites. Charming patio restaurant with outdoor pool and spa bath. 200 rooms.

67

LOS ANGELES – HOLLYWOOD AND WESTSIDE

Hotel Bel-Air ▯▯▯

701 Stone Canyon Road, Los Angeles, CA 90077
Tel. (310) 472 1211; 800 648 4097
Fax (310) 476 5890

The ultimate in luxury – lavishly appointed bungalows and villas, set in lush woodland and gardens, provide a truly pampered movie-star lifestyle. 92 rooms.

Best Western Sunset Plaza Hotel ▯▯

8400 Sunset Boulevard, West Hollywood, CA 90069
Tel. (213) 654 0750;
800 421 3652
Fax (213) 650 6146

A Californian-style family hotel on famous Sunset Strip. Bright, cheerful rooms with TV, VCR and refrigerator. Swimming pool and sundeck. 87 rooms.

Bevonshire Lodge Motel ▯

7575 Beverly Boulevard, Los Angeles, CA 90036
Tel. (213) 936 6154

Basic family motel with swimming pool and free parking, conveniently situated for Hollywood. Child-minding service available. 25 rooms.

Hotel del Capri ▯▯

10587 Wilshire Boulevard, Los Angeles, CA 90024
Tel. (310) 474 3511;
800 44-HOTEL
Fax (310) 470 9999

Charming and secluded hotel with pleasant, flower-fringed patio and swimming pool. 81 rooms.

Hollywood Celebrity Hotel ▯▯

1775 Orchid Avenue, Hollywood, CA 90028
Tel. (213) 850 6464;
800 222 7017

Quiet and intimate retreat near the Hollywood Bowl. Bright, spacious rooms with Art Deco motif. Price includes complimentary bottle of wine on arrival and breakfast.

Hollywood Roosevelt Hotel ▯▯▯

Hollywood Boulevard, Hollywood, CA 90028
Tel. (213) 466 7000;
800 950 7667
Fax (213) 462 8056

Located near the Mann's Chinese Theater (see p.53), this grand, forties-style hotel was the venue for the first Academy Awards ceremony. The atmospheric Cinegrill Supper Club is much frequented by movie and music-business people. 330 rooms.

Mondrian Hotel de Grande Classe |||

8440 Sunset Boulevard, West
Hollywood, CA 90069
Tel. (213) 650 8999;
800 525 8029
Fax (213) 650 5215

A colourful, geometric monument dedicated to the works of Dutch artist Piet Mondrian. Luxurious suites decorated with modern art enjoy fantastic views. Large pool, sauna, whirlpool and fitness centre. 220 suites.

The Peninsula Beverly Hills |||

9882 Little Santa Monica
Boulevard, Beverly Hills,
CA 90212
Tel. (310) 273 4888;
800 462 7899
Fax (310) 858 6663

Classical elegance and unrivalled luxury in this hotel in the heart of exclusive Beverly Hills. Rolls Royce limosine service, a rooftop pool and a romantic roof-garden restaurant. 184 rooms.

Saharan Motor Hotel |

7212 Sunset Boulevard,
Hollywood, CA 90046
Tel. (213) 874 6700
Fax (213) 876 2625

Reasonably priced motel with clean and comfortable accommo- dation, a swimming pool and free parking. 63 rooms.

Universal City Hilton and Towers |||

Universal Terrace Parkway,
Universal City, CA 91608
Tel. (818) 506 2500;
800-HILTONS
Fax (818) 509 2058

Gleaming 24-storey construction of chrome and glass overlooking Universal Studios. Tastefully dec- orated rooms with views. Glass- roofed atrium, café-bistro and Jap- anese restaurant. 449 rooms.

LOS ANGELES – COAST

Barnabey's ||-|||

3501 Sepulveda Boulevard,
Manhattan Beach, CA 90266
Tel. (310) 545 8466;
800 552 5285
Fax (310) 545 8621

Kitschy Victorian hotel furnished with antiques. Viennese restaurant with staff in period dress. Indoor pool. 128 rooms.

Cadillac Hotel |

401 Ocean Front Walk, Venice
Beach, CA 90291
Tel. (310) 399 8876
Fax (310) 399 4536

Great-value seafront accommoda- tion on offer in this restored art **69** deco landmark. There's a choice of private rooms or dormitory bunks. 41 rooms.

Hotel Carmel

201 Broadway, Santa Monica, CA 90401
Tel. (310) 451 2469
Offering good-value rooms right in the centre of Santa Monica, and situated close to the lively life on Santa Monica Pier and beach. 110 rooms.

Channel Road Inn

219 W. Channel Road, Santa Monica, CA 90402
Tel. (310) 459 1920
Fax (310) 454 9920
Rustic-style and romantic country house dating from 1910, complete with solid oak floors, wicker furniture and inviting four-poster beds. 14 rooms.

Malibu Beach Inn

22878 Pacific Coast Highway, Malibu, CA 90265
Tel. (213) 456 6444;
800 4-MALIBU
Fax (213) 456 1499
Exclusive mission-style hotel located right on Malibu beach. All rooms have their own balcony overlooking the sea. You couldn't have wished for a better setting. 47 rooms.

70

Seahorse Motel

233 N. Sepulveda Boulevard, Manhattan Beach, CA 90266
Tel. (213) 376 7951;
800 854 3380
Fax (213) 674 1137
Pleasant, friendly motel situated close to Manhattan Beach, as well as being convenient for the local airport. All rooms have air-conditioning and television. Heated swimming pool and coffee shop. 33 rooms.

SAN FRANCISCO

Adelaide Inn

5 Isadora Duncan Court, San Francisco, CA 94102
Tel. (415) 441 2261
Cheap and cheerful city-centre accommodation located close to lively Union Square. Guests have to share bathrooms, but are supplied with free coffee and doughnuts. 16 rooms.

Cow Hollow Motor Inn

2190 Lombard Street, San Francisco, CA 94123
Tel. (415) 921 5800
Fax (415) 922 8515
Comfortable motel near the Marina District, with its own restaurant and free parking. Rooms or self-catering suites are both available. 129 rooms.

Fairmont Hotel and Tower ▯▯▯

950 Mason Street, San Francisco, CA 94108
Tel. (415) 772 5000;
800 527 4727
Fax (415) 781 3929
Famous hilltop luxury hotel which boasts a fine, old lobby, complete with marble columns and sweeping panoramic views of San Francisco. 600 rooms.

Grant Plaza Hotel ▯

465 Grant Avenue, San Francisco, CA 94108
Tel. (415) 434 3883;
800 472 6899
Fax (415) 434 3886
Small but comfortable rooms, plus an ideal location on the edge of the colourful Chinatown district. 72 rooms.

Mark Hopkins InterContinental ▯▯▯

1 Nob Hill, San Francisco, CA 94108
Tel. (415) 392 3434;
800 327 0200
Fax (415) 421 3302
Enjoying the city's most prestigious address, this high-class hotel offers panoramic views of San Francisco from its famous 1940's rooftop bar, Top of the Mark (see p.29). 391 rooms.

Hotel Mark Twain ▯▯

345 Taylor Street, San Francisco, CA 94102
Tel. (415) 673 2332;
800 288 9246
Fax (415) 398 0733
Elegant little colonial-style hotel right in the heart of the Union Square district. 116 rooms.

Pacific Heights Inn ▯-▯▯

1555 Union Street, San Francisco, CA 94123
Tel. (415) 776 3310;
800 523 1801
Fax (415) 776 8176
Quiet, intimate hotel among the fashionable shops of Union Street. 40 rooms.

Phoenix Inn ▯▯

601 Eddy Street, San Francisco, CA 94109
Tel. (415) 776 1380
Fax (415) 885 3109
Large, pleasant rooms, overlooking a courtyard with swimming pool. Caribbean restaurant, free breakfast, free parking. 44 rooms.

Washington Square Inn ▯▯▯

1660 Stockton Street, San Francisco, CA 94133
Tel. (415) 981 4220;
800 388 0220
Fax (415) 397 7242

71

Pleasant, cosy spot offering bed and breakfast in the heart of the bohemian North Beach area. 15 rooms.

The Wharf Inn ▌▌
2601 Mason Street, San Francisco, CA 94133
Tel. (415) 673 7411; 800 548 9918
Fax (415) 776 2181
Comfortable small hotel situated in a popular tourist area, and conveniently located to get the cable-car to the city centre. Free parking. 50 rooms.

SAN DIEGO

Horton Grand Hotel ▐▐▐
311 Island Avenue, San Diego, CA 92101
Tel. (619) 544 1886
Fax (619) 239 3823
Classic, renovated turn-of-the-century hotel with staff dressed in full period costume, in the heart of San Diego's Gaslamp Quarter (see p.81). 132 rooms.

La Jolla Cove Motel ▌-▌▌
1155 Coast Boulevard, La Jolla, CA 92037
Tel. (619) 459 2621; 800 248 2683
Fax (619) 454 3522
Excellently priced motel offering rooms with balconies overlooking the ocean in upmarket La Jolla. Swimming pool, gymnasium. 120 rooms.

San Diego Marriot Hotel ▌▌
333 W. Harbour Drive, San Diego, CA 92101
Tel. (619) 234 1500; 800 228 9290
Fax (619) 234 8678
Plush rooms in gleaming high-rise hotel overlooking the yacht marina and Seaport Village (see p.81). 1,355 rooms.

US Grant Hotel ▐▐▐
326 Broadway, San Diego, CA 92101
Tel. (619) 232 3121; 800 237 5029
Fax (619) 232 3626
Classic grand hotel with rich wood panelling and leather upholstery, right in the heart of downtown San Diego. 280 rooms.

La Valencia ▐▐▐
1132 Prospect Street, La Jolla, CA 92037
Tel. (619) 454 0771; 800 451 0772
Fax (619) 456 3921
Old-style elegance and luxury overlooking La Jolla Cove. Sumptuous rooms, tropical patio, palm-fringed pool. 100 rooms.

Recommended Restaurants

California caters to all culinary tastes, offering everything from fried egg and hash browns at a cheap and cheerful diner to *pâté de foie gras* in a gourmet French restaurant, with all the world's cuisines in between. You can indulge your hunger at any time of day – most restaurants are open from morning until late in the evening (unless otherwise stated), and some are open 24 hours. Reservations are recommended for dinner in the more expensive restaurants, especially at weekends.

Below is a list of restaurants recommended by Berlitz. If you discover other places you think worthy of recommendation, we would be pleased to hear from you.

As a basic guide, the symbols below indicate the price of a three-course dinner for two, excluding wine, tax and tip:

I	below $35
II	$35–70
III	over $70

LOS ANGELES

Al Amir   II
5750 Wilshire Boulevard,
Hollywood
Tel. (213) 931 8740
Upmarket Middle Eastern restaurant, serving *falafel, tabbouleh,* shish kebab and other specialities.

Angeli Mare   II
Marina Market Place, 13455
Maxella Avenue, Marina del Rey
Tel. (310) 822 1984
Beautiful, modern Italian restaurant beside the yacht harbour. The menu ranges from pizza and pasta to gourmet seafood.

Benihana   II
38 N. La Cienega Boulevard,
Beverly Hills
Tel. (213) 655 7311
Enjoy steak, chicken and seafood prepared at your table by your own personal chef in this stylish Japanese restaurant. Closed Saturday and Sunday lunch.

Bernard's   III
Biltmore Hotel, 506 S. Grand
Avenue, Downtown
Tel. (213) 612 1580
This grand old dining room, complete with harpist, is an LA institution, serving gourmet French and Californian cuisine.

Café 50s

838 Lincoln Boulevard, Venice
Tel. (310) 399 1955
Burgers, milkshakes and malts in fifties diner decor, with table-top juke box and singing waitresses.

Chan Dara

11940 W. Pico Boulevard,
West Los Angeles
Tel. (213) 479 4461
Trendy and popular Thai restaurant. Two other branches at 1511 N. Cahuenga Boulevard, and 310 N. Larchmont Boulevard.

El Cholo

1121 S. Western Avenue,
Hollywood
Tel. (213) 734 2773
One of LA's original and best Mexican restaurants, with a Monday-night *mariachi* band. Lively and popular.

Cowboy Sushi

911 Broxton Avenue, Westwood
Tel. (310) 208 7781
Japanese sushi bar serving *tempura* and *teriyaki*, plus pasta and vegetarian dishes.

Gaylord

50 N. La Cienega Boulevard,
Beverly Hills
Tel. (310) 652 0163
Elegant pink/grey decor heralds this upmarket Indian restaurant. They offer the usual selection of korma, madras, vindaloo and tandoori dishes, served with a touch of class.

Gorky's Café

1716 N. Cahuenga Boulevard,
Hollywood
Tel. (310) 463 4060
Described as 'a Russian avant-garde café with working people's prices', serving hearty salads and sandwiches, *blinis*, pastries and *sauerkraut*. Set in the seedy part of Hollywood that will be familiar to fans of the singer Tom Waits.

Hard Rock Café

Beverly Center,
8600 Beverly Boulevard,
West Hollywood
Tel. (310) 276 7605
Loud rock music, wise-cracking waitresses, trendy teenagers queuing for tables, and the trademark Cadillac crashing through the ceiling. The food's good too – burgers, chilli, barbecues and salads.

Lawry's – The Prime Rib

100 N. La Cienega Boulevard,
Beverly Hills
Tel. (310) 652 2827
As the name suggests, this traditional restaurant serves the best

and juiciest ribs in town, carved at your table by attentive waiters.

Matteo's ▮▮▮
2321 Westwood Boulevard,
West Los Angeles
Tel. (310) 475 4521
Go star spotting at this plush and exclusive Italian restaurant occasionally frequented by some of Hollywood's more famous faces. Closed Monday.

Mon Kee's ▮-▮▮
679 N. Spring Street, Downtown
Tel. (213) 628 6717
Restaurant serving superb Cantonese seafood – choose your dinner from the tanks of live fish, crab and lobster.

Moustache Café ▮▮
8155 Melrose Avenue,
West Hollywood
Tel. (213) 651 2111
Trendy meeting place on stylish Melrose Avenue. Californian cuisine specialities include their delicious rack of lamb and famous chocolate soufflé.

Musso & Frank Grill ▮▮
6667 Hollywood Boulevard,
Hollywood
Tel. (213) 467 7788
This New York-style bar and grill is a local institution, still steeped in the atmosphere of 1940's Hollywood. You really haven't been to Hollywood until you've eaten out here!

L'Orangerie ▮▮▮
903 N. La Cienega Boulevard,
West Hollywood
Tel. (310) 652 9770
Beautiful and romantic French restaurant serving classic *nouvelle cuisine*. Jacket and tie, and reservations required.

Original Pantry Café ▮
877 S. Figueroa Street,
Downtown
Tel. (213) 972 9279
Huge, well-prepared helpings of good solid fare in this very popular veteran diner. Open 24 hours.

Pacific Dining Car ▮▮-▮▮▮
1310 W. Sixth Street, Downtown
Tel. (213) 483 6000
Classic popular steakhouse, established in 1921 and housed in a preserved railway dining saloon. Open 24 hours.

Rae's Diner ▮
2901 Pico Boulevard,
Santa Monica
Tel. (213) 828 7937
This traditional 50's diner is not a modern pastiche but the genuine article, complete with streetwise, **75**

uniformed waitresses and huge breakfasts.

Shanghai Red's ‖

13813 Fiji Way, Fisherman's Village, Marina del Rey
Tel. (310) 823 4522

Dine on the wooden terrace overlooking the marina, or indoors by an open fire in winter. Steak, ribs, fresh fish and shellfish.

Tail of the Pup ‖

329 N. San Vicente Boulevard, West Hollywood
Tel. (310) 652 4517

Famous 1920's hot-dog stand in the shape of a giant hot dog. A place of pilgrimage for photographers and hot-dog connoisseurs.

Tommy Tang's ‖

7473 Melrose Avenue, West Hollywood
Tel. (213) 651 1810

A famous and popular people-watching spot, serving excellent, inventive Thai cuisine. Try tiger prawns in champagne and coriander sauce, or squid with mint leaves and chilli.

El Torito Grill ‖

9595 Wilshire Boulevard, Beverly Hills
Tel. (310) 550 1599

76 Bargain Mexican and Southwest-

ern restaurant in the middle of Beverly Hills. Loud and lively.

Yang Chow ‖

819 N. Broadway, Downtown
Tel. (213) 625 0811

Spicy Szechuan cuisine served in the heart of Chinatown. Decor is bright and basic, but the food is exquisite.

SAN FRANCISCO

Bentley's Seafood Grill & Oyster Bar ‖

185 Sutter Street, Financial District
Tel. (415) 989 6895

Live crab and lobster and a dozen different varieties of oyster are on the menu daily.

Blue Light Café ‖

1979 Union Street, Pacific Heights
Tel. (415) 922 5510

Owned by rock star Boz Scaggs. Rock music and warehouse decor, with mesquite-grilled steaks and Maine lobster. Monday to Saturday dinner only; Sunday brunch.

Buena Vista Café ‖

2765 Hyde Street, North Beach
Tel. (415) 474 5044

Irish coffee was invented in this lovely old café by the Bay. Huge breakfasts; drinks are served until 2.00am.

Café Trieste |

609 Vallejo Street,
North Beach
Tel. (415) 392 6739

Fine old neighbourhood café, with wonderful pizzas and delicious coffee. The juke-box offers operatic classics, and at the weekend the Italian owners perform impromptu arias.

Campo Santo |

240 Columbus Avenue,
North Beach
Tel. (415) 433 9623

Mexican/Mayan meets California Cuisine in this great value restaurant. Traditional Yucatán dishes (chicken or beef flavoured with *achiote*, green tomatoes, chilli and sour orange) are given the stylish California treatment. Don't miss the mango ice-cream with tequila and lime sauce.

Chevy's |

150 Fourth Street at Howard,
SoMa
Tel. (415) 543 8060

Lively Mexican cantina with fresh traditional dishes. Wash down the delicious *fajitas* (sizzling steak or chicken) with an equally delicious frozen Margarita.

Cliff House ||–|||

1090 Point Lobos Avenue,
Ocean Beach
Tel. (415) 386 3330

Four dining rooms and two bars in a spectacular spot overlooking Ocean Beach, Seal Rocks and the Golden Gate, and specializing in seafood and California cuisine.

Corona Bar & Grill ||

88 Cyril Magnin Street,
Downtown
Tel. (415) 392 5500

Upmarket Mexican with Old West decor, serving fresh seafood and regional specialities.

Empress of China ||

838 Grant Avenue, Chinatown
Tel. (415) 434 1345

Luxurious Chinese restaurant decorated with Han Dynasty antiques. Great views of Telegraph Hill.

Fog City Diner ||

1500 Battery Street, North Beach
Tel. (415) 982 2000

A gleaming art deco American diner, with twists on traditional dishes. Very chic, very popular.

Iron Horse ||

19 Maiden Lane,
Union Square
Tel. (415) 362 8133

Upmarket Italian restaurant, with **77**

crisp white tablecloths, red roses, dark wood panelling and polished copper creating a cosy, romantic atmosphere. Try the sautéed scallops in saffron herb butter, or the roast Sonoma duck with cassis. Reservations recommended.

John's Grill ▊▊

63 Ellis Street at Powell,
Downtown
Tel. (415) 989 0069
Opened in 1908, this steak and seafood establishment was a favourite haunt of private eye Sam Spade in *The Maltese Falcon.*

Miss Pearl's ▊▊
Jam House

601 Eddy Street at Larkin,
Civic Center
Tel. (415) 775 5267
Trendy, Caribbean-style poolside restaurant with a fun atmosphere. Closed Sunday dinner.

Sirtaj ▊

48 Fifth Street, Downtown
Tel. (415) 957 0140
Delicious North Indian food – tandoori dishes, biryani, vegetable curries. Excellent buffet lunch.

Stars ▊▊▊

150 Redwood Alley, Civic Center
Tel. (415) 861 7827
A stylish gourmet restaurant and

oyster bar with distinctive and creative Californian cuisine on the menu. Closed Monday to Friday at lunchtime.

The Stinking Rose ▊

325 Columbus Avenue,
North Beach
Tel. (415) 781-ROSE
A lively and fun-filled Italian restaurant dedicated to all lovers of garlic. Features a range of classical dishes with just one thing in common – the garlic is seasoned with food, not the other way round!

Trader Vic's ▊▊▊

20 Cosmo Place, Downtown
Tel. (415) 776 2232
This high-society hangout has its own distinctive Polynesian theme. complete with tropical-style decor and exotic cocktails. Jacket and tie required. Dinner only.

Vesuvio ▊

255 Columbus Avenue,
North Beach
Tel. (415) 362 3370
This legendary café-bar was once a hangout of the famous 1950's 'Beat generation' (see p.21), and is still frequented by a laid-back, literary crowd today. Conveniently situated next to the City Lights Bookstore (see p.33).

Washington Square
Bar & Grill
1707 Powell Street,
North Beach
Tel. (415) 982 8123
Lively Italian-style bistro with lunchtime jazz sessions, offering steak, pasta, seafood and burgers.

SAN DIEGO

B Street Grill &
Jazz Bar
425 West B Street, Downtown
Tel. (619) 236 1707
Popular nightspot serving Californian cuisine. Steaks, seafood and Asian dishes. Live jazz Friday and Saturday.

Barnacle Bill's
1880 Harbour Island Drive,
Harbour Island
Tel. (619) 297 1673
Harbourside dining with fresh fish and seafood, clam chowder, steak and ribs and more.

Café Broken Yolk
3350 Sports Arena Boulevard,
Point Loma
Tel. (619) 226 0442
Open for breakfast and lunch only, and specializing in huge, tasty omelettes and other egg dishes. Another branch at 1851 Garnet Avenue, Pacific Beach.

Café del Rey Moro
House of Hospitality,
Balboa Park
Tel. (619) 234 8511
Beautiful terrace overlooking the gardens of Balboa Park. The menu is Southwestern, a mix of Mexican and Native American influences.

Casa de Bandini
2660 Calhoun Street,
Old Town
Tel. (619) 297 8211
Lovely Mexican restaurant housed in an adobe hacienda which dates back to 1829.

Corvette Diner
3946 Fifth Avenue, Hillcrest
Tel. (619) 542 1476
Classic American 50s-style diner. Specialities such as meat loaf and barbecue pork ribs.

Firehouse
Beach Café
722 Grand Avenue, Pacific Beach
Tel. (619) 272 1999
All meals served on the sun deck, in sight of the Pacific surf.

French Side of
the West
2202 Fourth Avenue, Hillcrest
Tel. (619) 234 5540
Romantic candlelit French restaurant with patio. Five-course menu

79

of gourmet cuisine at a very reasonable fixed price.

George's at the Cove · ‖–‖‖

1250 Prospect Street,
La Jolla
Tel. (619) 454 4244
One of San Diego's top restaurants, with fantastic ocean views. Seafood and steak dishes given the Californian touch – light, fresh and inventive.

La Gran Tapa · ‖–‖

611 B Street, Downtown
Tel. (619) 234 8272
Stylish Spanish restaurant with full menu of main courses as well as over 40 varieties of *tapas*.

Kung Food · ‖

2949 Fifth Avenue, Hillcrest
Tel. (619) 298 7302
Delicious vegetarian fare – try the mushroom and spinach lasagne followed by pumpkin pie.

Little Italy · ‖

4204 Voltaire Avenue,
Ocean Beach
Tel. (619) 225 9000
Classic family-run Italian restaurant, down to the red-checked tablecloths and Chianti bottles. Delicious food served in substantial portions.

Old Columbia Brewery & Grill · ‖–‖‖

1157 Columbia Street,
Downtown
Tel. (619) 234 2739
San Diego's oldest brewery provides 19 kinds of beer to wash down a dinner of steaks, burgers, grills, salads and seafood.

La Salsa · ‖

Level 3, Horton Plaza,
Broadway, Downtown
Tel. (619) 234 6906
Fast, no-frills Mexican restaurant, offering freshly prepared *tacos*, *burritos*, *enchiladas*, *fajitas*, etc.

Sibyl's Down Under · ‖

500 Fourth Avenue,
Downtown
Tel. (619) 239 9117
Lively restaurant offering Australian specialities such as alligator tails and barbecued prawns wrapped in bacon. Having dinner entitles you to free entry to the upstairs nightclub.

Su Casa · ‖–‖

6738 La Jolla Boulevard,
La Jolla
Tel. (619) 454 0369
Excellent Mexican seafood restaurant decorated like an 18th-century hacienda, with painted tiles, fireplace, and oak furniture.

San Diego

This is where California's recorded history began when, in 1542, Juan Rodríguez Cabrillo stepped ashore at Point Loma (see p.10). Today, San Diego is California's second largest city, home to a major naval base, and has been voted one of America's most desirable cities to live in. The climate is perfect, the beaches are beautiful, the revitalized downtown area is lively, and the city manages to avoid the air pollution and congestion which plague Los Angeles.

The modern city centre contains 16 blocks of preserved Victorian buildings – the **Gaslamp Quarter**. Here you can stroll along the red-brick pavements and admire the charming restored architecture from the turn-of-the-century while you browse among the shops, galleries, cafés and bars.

By contrast, **Horton Plaza**, on Broadway is one of the best modern shopping malls in the US, with five floors of shops and restaurants, open-air terraces and quirky decorations. Broadway ends at the harbour edge, where you can visit one of several 19th-century ships moored on the Embarcadero and belonging to the excellent **Maritime Museum**.

The city's pride and joy is the iron-hulled square-rigger *Star of India,* built in the Isle of Man in 1863. The *Star* is the oldest sailing ship that is still seaworthy, and she makes a celebratory cruise twice each summer. A brief walk along the waterfront leads to **Seaport Village**, a lively complex of shops, restaurants and galleries overlooking the harbour.

One of the best ways to appreciate San Diego's sparkling beauty is from the sea. You can take a **cruise** along the bay – boat trips leave from Harbor Drive, just south of the Maritime Museum – out past the man-made Harbor and Shelter Islands and around the tip of the Coronado peninsula (occupied by a US Naval Air Base – the film *Top Gun* was set in San Diego) to Point Loma out on the Pacific coast. The seemingly endless procession of **81**

The skyscrapers of downtown San Diego overlook the busy harbour and palm-lined promenade.

fishing boats, yachts and US Navy vessels makes for a fascinating tour.

The superb **Balboa Park** is situated right in the centre of town, offering wooded walks and cycle paths, not to mention a wealth of sports facilities. There are also several museums concentrated around El Prado (the Promenade), including the San Diego Museum of Art, the Museum of Man, the Natural History Museum, the Aerospace Historical Center, the Automotive Museum and the Reuben H Fleet Space Theater and Science Center.

The highlight of the park is the **San Diego Zoo**, one of the finest in the world. Established in 1922, the zoo was a pioneer in the use of moats, ravines, rocks and embankments rather than bars and cages, giving the animals as large, free and natural a living space as possible. It is famous for its Sumatran tigers and Malaysian sun bears as well as a colony of koala bears – the only breeding population outside Australia. You can enjoy a bird's-eye view of the zoo from the Skyfari aerial tramway, or take a guided tour bus. An extension of the zoo is located 30 miles (48km) north at the **San Diego Wild Animal Park**, where 2,500 animals, including zebra, lions, elephants, cheetahs and rhinoceros roam freely.

The oldest part of San Diego is situated about 3 miles (4.8km) north of the city centre in the area known as the **Old Town** (bounded by Juan, Congress, Twiggs and Wallace Streets). Here, in 1769, the European colonization of California commenced, beginning with the construction of Father Junípero Serra's Mission San Diego de Alcala. In this area of restored adobe buildings you can enjoy a rest under the palms and eucalyptus of Plaza Vieja, originally the town centre and bullfight arena before the Yankees arrived, browse among the stalls selling Mexican handicrafts, or eat at one of the many restaurants.

Cabrillo National Monument, situated on the Point Loma promontory (follow the signs south west on Rosecrans Street), celebrates the discoverer of San Diego Bay. You can walk the trails around the point, visit the Old Point Loma Lighthouse, and at low tide explore the tide pools for crabs, starfish, anemone and, if you are lucky, perhaps even the odd, elusive octopus. If you're there between December and March, watch out for migrating grey whales from the lookout point near the lighthouse.

Other aquatic pursuits can be enjoyed at **Mission Bay**, a first-class watersports centre and park. The bay is also home of the famous **Sea World** marine park, where you'll be able to watch performing three-ton killer whales. Children especially will enjoy the antics of the trained dolphins, sealions and otters.

San Diego's **beaches** are truly beautiful and remarkably unspoilt, stretching for some 27 miles (43km) up to the elegant suburb of **La Jolla** (pronounced 'la hoya', Spanish for **83** 'jewel'), whose centrepiece is the tiny rock basin of La Jolla Cove. The rocky coast to the south is marvellous for walking, and away from the ocean there are stylish shops and elegant restaurants to visit. The marine life of southern California is splendidly displayed in the **Stephen Birch Aquarium-Museum**, which is spectacularly sited on the hilltop above La Jolla. The view of the ocean from the terrace is magnificent.

The Mountains and the Deserts

If California's great outdoors is a religion, then its cathedrals are found in the Yosemite and Sequoia/Kings Canyon national parks, as well as the Death Valley National Monument. In these magnificent stretches of wilderness – the mountains of the Sierra Nevada, the huge, silent redwood forests, and the awe-inspiring emptiness of the desert – you can begin to recapture the adventurous spirit of the earliest American experience. These parks are, naturally, immensely popular with Californians and tourists alike, Yosemite more so than the others, but they all have ample room for everyone to make their escape from the crowds.

Certain regulations must be observed within national parks boundaries. There are strict speed limits, for the most part lower than on normal highways. It is forbidden to feed or otherwise interfere with the wild animals you encounter, hunting is illegal and fishing requires a state licence. Hikers intending to camp in the back country must first obtain a wilderness permit (see p.119).

Certain areas are closed to camping, and fires are severely restricted to designated areas (see p.89). None of the regulations is a real burden, however, as there are excellent public campsites, picnic areas and

84

*D*esert winds have sandblasted the base of this curious rock formation in Death Valley.

barbecue facilities to be found in all the parks.

YOSEMITE NATIONAL PARK

The centre of the park, where all the accommodation and facilities (not to mention crowds during summer) are concentrated, is the spectacular Yosemite Valley.

This scenic wonder is a perfect example of a glacier-carved canyon, with its sheer granite walls 3,000ft (914m) high plunging to a flat floor of woods and wild-flower meadows, enclosing the waters of the Merced River. Your 'base camp' could be a plush hotel room, more modest lodge accommodation, or even just a tent. From the valley meadows you can hike, bike (rentals at Yosemite Lodge or Curry Village) or take the shuttle bus to all the principal sights.

You can grade the hikes according to your fitness and experience – if in doubt, seek advice at the Visitor Center – but try at least one walk, in sturdy shoes, for the sheer exhilaration of making it to the end. The trail from Happy Isles to **Vernal Falls** is within the scope of any reasonably fit and healthy person, following a well-marked path through the pine trees, with easy gradients. The brilliant light and intoxicatingly clean air on the trail are a true delight, and the thundering falls, at their best during the spring snow melt, are awe-inspiring.

If you're feeling up to it, push on along the Mist Trail, past Emerald Pool, to **Nevada Falls**, and you'll begin to lose the crowds. Here you're on part of the John Muir Trail (see p.38), which heads past Merced Lake and on to the lovely Tuolumne Meadows up

*S*heer cliffs and spectacular waterfalls enclose the woods and meadows of Yosemite Valley.

in the high country. The final destination of the John Muir Trail is Mount Whitney, more than 200 miles (322km) away.

Less exhausting is a drive or shuttle-bus ride past Badger Pass (good skiing slopes in winter) to **Glacier Point** – 7,214ft (2,200m) above sea level. The view over the whole valley and the High Sierras beyond is totally breathtaking, as is the other way to get here – a steep, 4 mile (6.5km) hike up the Glacier Point Trail.

You can see Yosemite Creek drop half a mile from the opposite wall in two spectacular plunges, the Upper and Lower **Yosemite Falls**, and you'll get an outstanding view of the majestic Half Dome, a granite monolith sliced in two by the Ice Age glaciers. From here you may feel like leaving the bus and hiking back down to the valley, along the Panorama Trail via the Nevada and Vernal Falls, a trip of 8 miles (13km), all of it downhill!

Another hike, both beautiful and easy, goes out to **Mirror Lake**, tucked beneath the vertical north-west face of Half **87**

Dome. This is especially good during spring or early summer when the waters are perfectly still in the early morning, capturing the most breathtaking colours from the trees and the cliffs of Mount Watkins behind it.

SEQUOIA AND KINGS CANYON NATIONAL PARKS

These two parks lie adjacent to each other, and are usually visited together – one entrance ticket covers both. The main attractions are their giant sequoias, many of them approaching 3,000 years old, and the spectacular rock scenery of Kings Canyon. The forests offer a gorgeous array of dogwoods, sugar pines and white firs, and a rich flora of orange leopard lily, lupine, bracken fern, chinquapin and white corn lily.

Start at the Visitor Center at Lodgepole or Grant Grove, where you can pick up a map and information about the best forest walks and back-country hikes, and perhaps watch their

interesting documentary film about the sequoias.

The best introduction to the forest is **Congress Trail**. It's an easy 2-mile (3km) walk, but worth lingering over for a couple of hours to absorb the beauty of the largest living creations in nature. The trail begins at the **General Sherman Tree**, the biggest of them all. Measuring 275ft (84m), 103ft (31m) round its base and still growing, it's the largest living organism in the world. Reaching up for light well above the rest of the forest, the first branches start 130ft (40m) above the ground.

Another beautiful walk, and by no means an exhausting one, is out to **Crescent Meadow**, passing on the way such venerable trees as the Bear's Bathtub, the Shattered Giant and the Chimney.

If you want to get away and discover the real back country, carry on along the High Sierra Trail for 11 miles (18km) beyond Crescent Meadow to get to **Bearpaw Meadow**. This is not too formidable a hike, and the meadow has a rudimentary campsite. The nearby lake and streams offer good fishing, especially for trout, and you'll have a fair chance of spotting some of the park's wildlife too – bobcats, coyotes, golden eagles, black bear, spotted skunk and cougar.

Majestic redwoods tower high above the road in Sequoia National Park.

Good and Bad Fires

While hiking in Sequoia National Park you'll come across the scars of past fires on some of the giant redwoods. These are the result of wildfires (accidental or natural, started by lightning), prescribed fires (deliberately started by park rangers) or prescribed natural fires (started by natural causes but allowed to burn out). You may even encounter a prescribed fire in action. It will be well marked with signs telling you, 'Do not panic, do not report, do not extinguish.'

In fact, sequoias *need* fires in order to survive. The fire kills harmful parasitic insects and fungi, and burns away excess undergrowth that can prevent young trees from sprouting. The sequoia has a thick bark that insulates the growing part of the trunk from fire damage. The deeply fluted bark can be more than 2ft (61cm) thick, and you will see many trees with a hollowed scar caused by fires long past. These trees still flourish hundreds of years later. The rangers' prescribed fires are simply good husbandry.

DEATH VALLEY NATIONAL MONUMENT

Of all the wonders of California, the **high desert** is perhaps the greatest surprise. This is no monotonous expanse of sand dunes but a beautiful variegated land full of colour and space. In summer it's a bizarre landscape of jagged rock and gravel, naked mountains and salt lakes, baked and shimmering in the desert heat. Go there in winter and you may see drifts of spring flowers blooming in the wake of the sparse rains that make it over the snow-dusted Panamint Mountains in the west. Unhidden by vegetation, the colours of the naked rocks – brick red, ochre, green, and purple-brown – are dramatically deepened at sunset and dawn, creating unforgettable views.

Don't be put off by the name **Death Valley**. It is a legacy of the bitter hardships endured by Gold Rush hopefuls who set out to cross the desert from Arizona and Nevada. Some never made it.

Today's travellers, however, are well catered for, with motels and campsites at Furnace Creek and Stovepipe Wells. Begin at the **Furnace Creek**

*B*are rock and wind-whipped sand – the desolate landscape of Death Valley.

Visitor Center, where you can pick up maps and information on the road conditions, hiking trails and general desert safety. Driving is the only way to get around, but remember that distances are great, and petrol (gas) stations few and far between. Make sure your car is in good mechanical condition,

and that the tank is full before you begin each day's tour. Also, carry spare water in case the radiator boils over.

Get up at dawn – you won't regret it – and drive out to **Zabriskie Point**. As the sun rises behind you, the light hits Tucki Mountain and the tips of the Panamints to the west before plunging into the valley's primeval salt lake far below. Continue to **Dante's View** (altitude 5,745ft/1,750m), where you can look out westward to Wildrose, Bennett and Telescope peaks and, on a good, clear day, to Mount Whitney (14,495ft/4,418m) which is 85 miles (137km) away. Down in the valley in front of you lies the salty puddle called **Badwater** – at 282ft (86m) below sea level, the lowest point in the western hemisphere.

The crazed and pinnacled surface of the salt-caked lake bed has earned it the nickname of **Devil's Golf Course**. Take a walk out across that glaring expanse of baked salt – the atmosphere of desolation is almost exhilarating. Look closer at the salt and you'll discover that the expansion of the crystallizing salts has heaved it into bizarre funnels, swirls and other intricate patterns.

Heading back towards Furnace Creek lies **Artist's Drive**, where the road (one way only from south to north) carves its path through a canyon of multi-coloured rocks, culminating in the very aptly named Artist's Palette. Here, oxidization has turned the rocks bright mauve, ochre, green, vermilion, turquoise and purple.

Death Valley was an irresistible magnet for prospectors, who once scoured the hills and canyons for signs of copper, lead, gold and silver. Thus the mountains are riddled with old mines and exploratory shafts, but only a few struck paydirt. You can explore the remains of the **Keane Wonder Mine** on the east side of the valley and the ghost town of **Skidoo** in the west, where $3 million of gold was dug out over a period of two years.

At the northern boundary of Death Valley, 45 miles (72km) from Furnace Creek, lies the remarkable **Scotty's Castle**, a luxuriously furnished twenties Spanish-style mansion which rises improbably from the bed of Grapevine Canyon. It was built for a Chicago millionaire, Albert Johnson, who spent his winters prospecting for gold with his partner and friend, Walter Scott, known to all as 'Death Valley Scotty'. Guided tours take you round the lavish interior, and you can wander at will around the grounds. Nearby lies **Ubehebe Crater**, the spectacular result of a volcanic explosion. A short trail will lead you down to the floor of the crater.

Excursion to Las Vegas

Inland from the urban jungle of LA lies the dry and desolate expanse of the **Mojave Desert** a vast, empty landscape that stretches 200 miles (322km) to the Nevada border. Interstate Highway 15 slashes through the desert and across the state line, heading straight for the neon sprawl of Las Vegas, the glittering city dedicated to the pursuit of the fast buck. The city grew out of a stopover at a natural oasis, and burgeoned after Nevada's legalization of gambling in 1931. Today, punters converge on Vegas from all over America. Many are there for a bit of fun and titillation, prepared to lose a few bucks at roulette or blackjack; others arrive with serious dollar signs in their eyes, desperately hoping to hit the jackpot. The only real winners are the casinos of course – you just can't beat the house.

The famous focal point of Las Vegas is **The Strip**, 4 miles (6.5km) of Las Vegas Boulevard crammed with huge casino and hotel complexes. Each is designed according to some fanciful theme – **Circus Circus**, with clowns for attendants and a trapeze act high above the tables; the **Tropicana**, with its island paradise of coconut palms and dusky maidens; the **MGM Grand**, with the characters from *The Wizard of Oz* – all dazzlingly lit with floodlights and garish neon signs.

93

The best time to arrive in Las Vegas is at sunset, when the city lights loom out of the desert darkness. For the same reason night-time is the best time to roam The Strip, when the lights are brightest and the tables at their liveliest. Apart from the decor, the casinos are pretty much alike – admission is free, and they're open 24 hours a day, 365 days a year. There are serried ranks of one-armed bandits near the doors, the delights of roulette, black-jack, craps and Keno further

Casinos line the glittering gulch of Las Vegas Boulevard – the world-famous 'Strip' – there to tempt.

in, and everywhere huge television screens showing horse-racing and other big sporting events from all over the country. For the bewildered, there are free booklets explaining how best to lose your money at the various tables, and free blackjack lessons in the afternoons. You will notice there are no clocks or windows in the casinos – the management want you to lose track of time. But there are plenty of ATMs (Automated Teller Machines) where you can carry on emptying your bank account when the chips run out.

There are also alternatives to gambling – the big casinos offer live stage shows, with all kinds of entertainment, from major singing stars like Liza Minnelli and Frank Sinatra, to leggy extravaganzas like the Folies Bergères, to world title boxing matches. You'll notice, too, the numerous 'wedding chapels' where you can get married in about 10 minutes for a flat $50 fee, 'witnesses extra', and then spend your honeymoon in the adjoining motel. If it doesn't last, there's

From Meadows to Mammon

Las Vegas is Spanish for 'the meadows', and was named by the Spanish explorers of the early 1800s who found good pastures here at the edge of the Mojave Desert. Today over 21 million people visit Las Vegas annually to try their luck on the gaming tables and slot machines, to the tune of $3 billion a year.

If you fancy having a go, but have never played the tables before, a number of casinos offer a free introductory session on the various games and rules, in the hope that you'll then go off and fritter away your hard-earned dollars. However, even in the kingdom of Mammon there are restrictions – anyone under the age of 21 is prohibited from entering a casino or purchasing alcohol.

a place just along the street where you can get divorced just as easily – for a slightly higher fee, of course. **95**

What to Do

Sports

In California you can enjoy all kinds of sports, from jogging to hang-gliding, from cycling to snorkelling, and in winter you can even squeeze a morning's surfing and an afternoon's downhill skiing into one day. The Golden State is a paradise for outdoor activities, but we start with what must be California's favourite.

WATERSPORTS

If you get no other exercise while you're in California, it would be difficult to go without at least one day swimming at the beach. It's no coincidence that most of the United States' champion swimmers come from southern California. In the middle-class neighbourhoods it seems that every other house has its own swimming pool – from the air you see the mass of turquoise blobs as you fly into the airport.

California is a true paradise for watersports enthusiasts of all shapes and sizes.

Surfing, snorkelling, scuba diving, sailing, fishing, water-skiing and windsurfing can all be enjoyed at various points on the coast. Everyone has their favourite beach or bay, and some are better for one sport than another.

Good **beaches** in the San Diego area can be found at Silver Strand, Mission and La Jolla. In Los Angeles the best beaches are Redondo, Santa Monica, Hermosa, Manhattan, Venice, Malibu and Zuma.

One warning to swimmers further north, however – at the resort village of Carmel-by-the-Sea the beach is great for sunbathing, but strong undercurrents make the sea too dangerous for swimming.

Surfing

Surfers have been riding California's waves since 1907, and

it's still incredibly popular. According to the American experts, California rates second only to Hawaii for surfing, though some Australians of course may well be justified in arguing the point.

The best waves for surfing are to be found at Malibu on Point Duma and Surfrider at Santa Monica State Beach, north of the pier, and there are also good waves at La Jolla on Windansea and Boomer beaches. **97**

Snorkelling

Good snorkelling is to be found at Abalone Cove on the Palos Verdes Peninsula south of LA, at Corona del Mar near Newport Beach and at La Jolla Cove, San Diego. At all these beaches you will also find windsurfing and waterskiing, the latter being good, too, up north at Sausalito and Tiburon.

Scuba Diving

There is marvellous scuba diving among the kelp forests of the coastline. Some of the best centres are Monterey, Santa Barbara and La Jolla, all of which offer equipment rental and instruction.

Sailing

When it comes to sailing, San Diego is the state's unchallenged leader. Every conceivable kind of vessel, from the smallest rowing boat to the largest ocean-going yacht, can be seen in the marinas of Mission Bay and around Shelter Island and Harbor Island in San Diego Bay. The sheltered waters of Mission Bay are an ideal nursery for learning the basics of boat handling, while for the more experienced and adventurous the wide Pacific waits outside. Sailing instruction and boat rentals – rowing boats, power boats, sailing dinghies and yachts – are all available at Mission Bay, San Diego; Marina del Rey, Los Angeles; and at Sausalito, near San Francisco.

Fishing

Sea angling can be enjoyed from the rocks and piers along the coastline, while deep-sea fishing is available from all of the sailing harbours listed above.

SPORTS ASHORE

Tennis

Public courts are plentiful and cheap – just a few dollars an hour, even in Beverly Hills (at Roxbury Park, 401 S Roxbury Drive). The best of the municipal courts, floodlit at night, are to be found in San Francisco's Golden Gate Park, Los Angeles' Griffith Park and Balboa Park in San Diego, but usually you will find dozens of courts within walking distance of hotels, or within the grounds of hotels themselves.

Golf

Golf is much cheaper here than in Europe, with courses all around the major cities – Griffith Park in Los Angeles, for instance, has two 18-hole courses, and San Francisco's Golden Gate has one 9-hole course.

The golf capital of California, however, is without doubt the Monterey Peninsula, with 18 full-sized courses, half of them public. The other nine, which include world-famous tournament courses, can be played through arrangements with certain hotels in the area. The best of the public courses are the Del Monte in Monterey, the Pebble Beach, Spyglass Hill on the peninsula, and the Rancho Canada in Carmel. There are also good-golf courses in Palm Springs.

Running

In this fitness-crazy state you can run just about everywhere, best of all barefoot along the beach. Sports stores will attempt to sell you all manner of 'essential' running equipment – *haute couture* tracksuits and shoes, lap timers, sweatbands, pedometers – but all you really need is a good pair of running shoes and a towel.

Cycling

Cycling is very well-catered for, especially in San Diego, Santa Barbara and Monterey. Even LA has a coastal cycle path which goes from Santa Monica to Redondo Beach. There are miles of pleasant cycle paths in Griffith Park, LA, and Golden Gate Park, San Francisco. More adventurous cyclists can savour the delights of mountain biking down the steep trails of Mount Tamalpais in Marin County. Bicycle rentals are available at **99**

Mission Beach, San Diego; Venice Beach, LA; and Golden Gate Park, San Francisco.

Roller-skating

If you enjoy nursing grazed knees and elbows, you might like to emulate the local inhabitants and try a spot of roller-skating, using in-line skates, or roller-blades, which have the wheels all in a row instead of one at each corner. Venice Beach is the place to go – you can rent skates right on the boardwalk. Just so long as you don't object to being shown up by the resident ten-year-old experts ...

BACK-COUNTRY SPORTS

Fishing

Trout fishing in the Sierra Nevada is one of the many outdoor pursuits you can enjoy in the national parks. Obtain a fishing licence and head out on a camping expedition along **100** the Tuolumne River in Yose-

mite, or try Merced Lake, a 3-day trip from Yosemite Valley. In Sequoia there are also good fishing trips to take from Bearpaw Meadow.

Hiking

There are trails to suit all ages and levels of fitness and experience, from a one-hour hike along a signposted valley path to multi-day expeditions along the John Muir Trail at Yosemite to Mount Whitney.

Horse riding

Yosemite and Sequoia are both great places for horse riding, with rental stables near the main hotels and lodges.

Skiing

In the winter, first-class cross-country skiing is available in Yosemite Valley and its surrounding wild country. There are also downhill skiing areas at Badger Pass near Yosemite and in Squaw Valley near Lake Tahoe. Other popular ski resorts are the Mammoth Lakes in the Eastern Sierra and Big Bear Lake, a few hours drive from LA.

For a full list of skiing resorts, ask at a Visitor Information Center (see p.140) for the Winter Sports Guide.

Rock climbing

Yosemite Valley is one of the best and most famous rock climbing centres in the world, and climbers flock from all over the country to take up the challenge of its sheer 3,000ft (914m) granite walls. If you're tempted, the Yosemite School of Mountaineering offers introductory courses.

SPECTATOR SPORTS

Big events in the California sporting calendar include the Bob Hope Desert Golf Classic at Palm Springs (February); the Long Beach Grand Prix in

LA (March); the LA Marathon (March); and the San Francisco Marathon (July).

American football

Europeans who visit between August and December should take the opportunity to experience the atmosphere of an American football game. The San Diego Chargers, the Los Angeles Rams and the Los Angeles Raiders all have large and faithful followings, but the San Francisco 49ers were the

Cars are by no means the only form of speedy transport to be found in California.

most consistently successful Californian team during the 1980s, winning the Superbowl championship three times during the decade.

At college level, where the antics of the fans and cheerleaders are far more highly spirited than at the professional matches, the team with the strongest tradition is the Trojans, from USC (the University of Southern California), LA.

Baseball

Major league baseball is represented by the San Francisco Giants, the Oakland As and the LA Dodgers, though you would have to be a real aficionado to be able to sit through all nine innings. For a foreigner unfamiliar with the sport the ritual is worth at least an hour. The season lasts from April to October.

Cyclists explore the miles of beautiful wooded trails in the stunning surroundings of Yosemite Valley.

Basketball

Basketball is as popular in California as in the rest of the US – the season lasts from October to April. Probably the best-known team is the Los Angeles Lakers, whose number-one fan, actor Jack Nicholson, often attends their games.

Horse-racing

California's principal horse-racing meetings include the San Juan Capistrano Handicap (mid-April) at Santa Anita, and the Breeders Cup Classic (early November) at Hollywood Park, both in LA.

Entertainment

NIGHTLIFE

If you want to enjoy a good night out on the town, then San Francisco definitely has the edge over Los Angeles. The 'City by the Bay' is one of the world's classic drinking towns, crammed with boisterous bars, cosy cafés, sophisticated bistros, and lively nightclubs, not to mention jumping jazz joints. SoMa, Broadway, Polk Street and Columbus Avenue are good places to sample the bars and clubs.

San Francisco nightlife is managing to shake off a reputation for sleaze that built up in the 1960s and 70s – after all, this is the town that gave the world the first topless (and ultimately bottomless) bar-room dancer. Until recently, the finer assets of Carol Doda, the original topless dancer, were immortalized in garish neon at the intersection of Broadway and Columbus.

In Los Angeles the clubs are perhaps trendier, and certainly more expensive, but the sheer size of LA makes a car pretty much a necessity for cruising the nightspots (taxi fares will be very expensive for more than a short trip). The best areas for clubs and bars are around Hollywood, on Sunset Boulevard, near the UCLA campus in Westwood Village, and out by the coast. Santa Monica is one area where you can explore on foot, and there **103** are many attractive bars along Main Street and at the ocean ends of Wilshire and Santa Monica boulevards.

MUSIC

Classical

The Los Angeles Philharmonic Orchestra gives excellent concerts at the Dorothy Chandler Pavilion in the Music Center, and performs open-air 'Symphonies under the Stars' at the Hollywood Bowl (in the summer only). There are also regular recitals and concerts at Royce Hall on the campus of UCLA. The San Francisco Symphony performs at the Davies Hall from December to May, and gives concerts of lighter music in the summer at the Civic Auditorium.

Jazz

For more uplifting entertainment, try to take in some of that quintessentially American musical style – jazz. San Francisco has many bars, restaurants and clubs offering live jazz in the evening, and occasionally at Sunday lunchtime too – 'jazz brunch' is becoming something of a Sunday institution on the west coast. Try Kimball's Jazz Club at 300 Grove Street, or the more intimate Jack's Bar at 1601 Fillmore, or take a look in the free weekly listings paper *Bay Area Music*.

Opera and Ballet

The San Francisco Opera is one of the best in the country, and attracts leading international singers to its 3-month season beginning in mid-September. The Curran Theatre holds Spring Opera in March for new American singers.

The San Francisco Ballet has its main season at the Opera House in the spring, but also puts on performances during December.

THEATRE

Theatre gets too much competition from the cinema in Los Angeles to reach a consistently

*B*ig wheels and carousels are among the plentiful fairground attractions to be found at Santa Monica pier.

high level, but occasionally there are good visiting companies at the Ahmanson Theatre and at the Shubert Theatre in Century City.

San Francisco has a good repertory company, the American Conservatory Theater, performing a varied programme from October to May at the Geary Theater as well as one major production throughout the summer months.

CINEMA

In LA, the home of the film industry, there are three big annual events: an international film festival in April, spon- **105** sored by the American Film Institute; a European film festival in June; and a festival of comic films in September.

The summit of Hollywood hype and glitter is attained in April, when the Oscars, or the Academy Awards, are handed out to the film industry's golden lights. The ceremony takes place at the Dorothy Chandler Pavilion, and admission is by invitation only to members of the Motion Pictures Academy, nominees and their friends. If you're not one of them you can still go along and watch the stars arrive.

For serious film-goers, the best cinemas in LA are around Westwood, but the old movie palaces still go in Hollywood. Summer is the season for any new releases, giving you the chance to see films that won't open back home until autumn or around Christmas.

San Francisco's film festival runs from mid-April to early May at the Kabuki Cinemas in Japantown and the Pacific Film Archives in Berkeley. Both attract major international productions.

Shopping

For many years California has been a trendsetter for casual clothes, gadgets, rollerskates, surfboards, skateboards, boogie boards (for bodysurfing in the ocean), basketball shoes, and mountain bikes. Most of the goods on sale in Californian stores are available elsewhere, but the latest innovations will be here first.

SAN FRANCISCO

The main downtown shopping district centres around **Union Square**, with all major New York and West Coast department stores represented.

There is a special emphasis on the classic tailoring of the more conservative kinds of clothing stores, such as Brooks Brothers. The shopping centres of **The Cannery** at **Fisherman's Wharf** as well as **Ghirardelli Square** are aimed at San Francisco's younger set. Both of these are situated in pleasant surroundings with plenty of open-air cafés, bookstores and restaurants.

The **Embarcadero** shopping centre, known as Rockefeller West, is a triple-level complex of shops, sculpture courts, restaurants, walkways and bridges that promises a full day's shopping. You might consider buying a ten-gallon cowboy hat – San Francisco claims that it makes the best.

North Beach is noteworthy above all for its bookshops. One of them, the City Lights Bookstore (see p.33), is a local institution and a Mecca for the followers of the Beat generation. There is more sophisticated shopping – for art and antiques, fashion, and designer goods – along **Union Street** west of Van Ness and on Polk Street south from Union.

LOS ANGELES

All of California's major cities have elegant shopping districts, but the most spectacular is **Rodeo Drive** in Beverly Hills (it was here that Richard Gere dressed Julia Roberts in the film *Pretty Woman*). But LA has other stylish shopping districts, too: **Wilshire Boulevard** (ironically named after the eccentric socialist Gaylord Wilshire), **Century City**, near Westwood Village; and **Melrose Avenue** in West Hollywood. Of the great department

Souvenirs Mexican style can be tracked down in LA's Olvera Street market.

107

stores, I Magnin's on Wilshire (formerly Bullock's) is a local institution.

Hollywood, not surprisingly, is the place to track down movie memorabilia – original posters that are now valued collectors' items, screenplays, pin-ups, biographies and film-related books. There are also excellent cinema bookshops along Hollywood Boulevard.

Flea markets are set up on the waterfront at **Venice** Beach and, on Saturday at Pasadena's **Rose Bowl**. You should also

look out for the **garage sales** that are regularly advertized in residential areas, where families clear out any unwanted articles – everything from old tennis rackets to kitchen gadgets. You can often pick up some truly amazing bargains, as well as pieces of Americana that may mean more to foreigners than they do to their American owners.

RESORT SHOPPING

All the seaside resorts along the coast have attractive boutiques, but the best are at Sausalito, Carmel, Newport Beach and La Jolla. At Pebble Beach, near the golf courses of the Monterey Peninsula, you will also find a magnificent collection of golf and other sports equipment.

Note that a sales tax will be added to the price of *all* your purchases (see p.131).

A great personal gift, have a T-shirt designed and coloured while you wait at Venice Beach.

Eating Out

The good things to eat while you're staying in California are the simple things. Thanks to the fertile, irrigated soils of the Central Valley, the beneficent climate, and the rich fisheries of the Pacific Ocean, the fruit, vegetables, meat and fish produced here are fresher, tastier and usually bigger than almost anywhere else in the United States.

WHERE TO EAT

There is an enormous variety of places where you can sample all this delicious produce. California offers every kind of eating place from very expensive, internationally renowned restaurants to the most humble of hot-dog stands, with all manner of things in between.

Not only is there the highly innovative and tasty home-grown Californian cuisine, but also a huge range of ethnic cuisines introduced by immigrants from all over Europe and Asia who have flocked to the coast in large numbers over the years.

MEAL TIMES

You will find that many restaurants are open at all hours of the day and night. Breakfast is usually available from 7am to 10am, though British visitors may be surprised to discover that some restaurants continue to serve pancakes, waffles and egg dishes throughout the day. Lunch extends from 11am to 2.30pm, and during the week downtown restaurants are jam-packed with office workers. Dinner is served from 5.30pm to 10.30pm or thereabouts.

EATING HABITS

For European visitors, Californian eating habits may need some introduction. As soon as you sit down for breakfast you're likely to see the waitress advancing on you with a pot of coffee. If you don't want coffee, better say so immediately. The coffee will be weak by European standards, but your cup is refilled several **109** times, at no extra charge. If you're having fried eggs, remember to specify 'sunny side up' (cooked on one side only, with a runny yolk) or 'over easy' (turned and then cooked lightly on top). There's also a choice of different toasts – white, whole wheat or rye.

At lunch and dinner, salad is usually served before the main dish, not with it. Salad dressings are often surprising concoctions not familiar to every European palate. If you want a simple dressing you can always order oil, vinegar and a little mustard and mix your own vinaigrette. You may find in some restaurants that you are offered a cocktail before, during and after the meal – cocktails are not necessarily considered apéritifs – but you can always order wine immediately if you prefer.

Service in even the cheapest of diners is invariably friendly and efficient. This is because waiting staff depend on tips for a large part of their income. Remember this at the end of a meal, and leave 15-20 percent of the bill. Leaving nothing

would be considered very rude (and may result in the waiter/waitress asking you what the problem was).

CALIFORNIAN SPECIALITIES

Salads

Salads are a great favourite in the healthy, clean-living state of California. One of the best is raw spinach with cream and crisp crumbs of bacon. Avocados are popular too, served with vinaigrette or filled with seafood. Each chef claims his or her own secret recipe for the famous Caesar salad, which for purists is romaine (Cos) lettuce, hard-boiled egg, garlic, olive oil, Parmesan cheese and lemon juice.

Seafood

Seafood is especially good in San Francisco and Monterey, and around San Diego. There is superb seabass, swordfish and tuna, including the delicious long-fin tuna known as

Make the most of the Californian climate and enjoy breakfast on the beach.

albacore. Seafood this fresh is at its best prepared simply.

While Boston makes chowder from clams, San Francisco uses tasty abalone (also eaten raw) and oysters. Some traditional San Francisco restaurants serve up a dish called Hangtown Fry, an omelette with ham and oysters which is said to have been requested as a last breakfast by a convicted murderer in the Gold Rush.

Crab is a great delicacy on the West Coast. Crab Louis, a salad of crab meat, eggs, lettuce and tomatoes, is served with a dressing of mayonnaise, chilli sauce and horseradish (connoisseurs insist on capers, too.) Jumbo shrimp (prawns) are wonderful barbecued in the shell with garlic.

Meat

The best bet among meat dishes is beef: steaks in a variety of cuts including porterhouse, **111** filet mignon sirloin and minute steak. Roast prime rib of beef, a marvellous (vast!) luxury, is served with enormous baked Idaho potatoes, while barbecued spare ribs, both beef and pork, have a devoted following. Hamburgers come as large patties served with onion, relish and a loaf of sourdough bread. Order them like steak, rare, medium or well done.

Desserts

In this land of abundant fresh fruit, desserts are a delight – strawberries, peaches, grapefruit and grapes are all a little larger and sweeter than you can find back home. If, on the other hand, you fancy something a little more decadent for dessert, try the strawberries thickly coated with chocolate that are served in some Beverly Hills establishments.

Best of all is the dairy icecream, available in dozens of delicious flavours. You can make a whole meal of it in one of the many ice-cream parlours in Westwood. Rather less fattening is frozen yoghurt,

also available in a wide range of flavours. Don't miss that great national dish, apple pie served *à la mode* – with icecream on top.

FOREIGN CUISINE

Italian

California's cooking has been greatly enriched by the ethnic diversity of its immigrants. Most of San Francisco's Italians didn't bother to stop off in New York or Chicago, they headed straight for the West Coast, and their restaurants in North Beach are among the best in the country. One Italian speciality is San Francisco's superb answer to bouillabaisse – a thick fish soup known as *cioppino*, more fish than soup, and containing every available shellfish from the Pacific.

Chinese

In San Francisco, Chinese cuisine is as good as you can find outside China itself. One of the great pleasures of visiting

San Francisco's Chinatown is sampling a *dim sum* lunch of egg rolls, meat dumplings, deep-fried sweet potatoes and chopped mushrooms served in wedges of rice pastry, accompanied by pots of sauce.

Those restaurants in and around Grant Avenue can offer all the variations of Chinese regional cooking – Peking, Szechuan, Shanghai, as well as the ubiquitous Cantonese. It's worth phoning a day in advance to order a whole Peking duck, glazed with honey and roasted with spring onions. This subtle delicacy contrasts sharply with the spicy smoked duck you will find in a Szechuan or Hunan restaurant. In addition, don't overlook the seafood specialities such as steamed seabass with spring onion, black beans, garlic, ginger and sesame oil, or Szechuan shrimp, always served piping hot – in both senses of the word.

*S*alads are a big favourite in health-conscious California.

Mexican

The best Mexican restaurants are to be found along La Cienega Boulevard in Los Angeles, and in San Diego. Mexican eating houses offer an array of bite-sized food to take away – crispy *tacos*, moist *tostadas* and *tortillas* stuffed with shredded beef or chicken, grated cheese, avocado and re-fried beans. The best dishes are quite difficult to manage **113**

comfortably standing up. Take a table in a restaurant to enjoy dishes such as *sopa de mazorca con pollo* (chicken and corn soup), *carne de puerco en adobo* (pork in chilli sauce) or 114 *mole poblano* (chicken with sesame seeds, chilli, peanuts, raisins, and a chocolate sauce).

Jewish

Big favourites in Hollywood are the Jewish delicatessens

*F*or a classic American combination, try a hot-dog and mustard washed down with a refreshingly cold Coors beer.

found on Fairfax Avenue and, more expensively, in Beverly Hills. Jewish cuisine features the Eastern European *borscht* (beetroot and cabbage soups with sour cream), *gefilte* fish (minced fish balls) and *lox* (cured and smoked salmon). *Blintzes*, a crisper version of the Russian *blini*, are little pancakes folded over minced meat as an appetizer, or filled with sweetened cream cheese as a dessert. Corned beef and pastrami (spicy smoked beef, Romanian-style) make great sandwiches; they're usually served on rye bread with potato salad and pickled cucumbers.

For dessert try some cheesecake – deliciously thick and creamy, with a sweet, cakecrumb crust and a generous topping of strawberries, blueberries or cherries.

Health Food

One cuisine that cuts across all ethnic lines is health food – always very popular in fitness-conscious California. Virtually every restaurant offers a selection of healthy and/or meat-free dishes. There are plenty of specialist health-food and vegetarian restaurants around Venice and Santa Monica in LA and in Mill Valley, north of San Francisco, which serve delicious and inventive salads, and every imaginable fruit and vegetable juice.

DRINKS

California is proud of its **wines**, and with good reason. Grapes have been grown in the **115**

Napa and Sonoma valleys to the north of San Francisco since the mid-19th century, and Californian wines compare favourably with the best that Europe can produce.

The wines are distinguished by the European grape variety from which they are grown. Red wines include *Cabernet Sauvignon*, *Pinot Noir* and *Zinfandel*, whose origin puzzles the experts. The principal whites are *Chardonnay*, *Sauvignon Blanc*, *Gewürztraminer* and *Riesling*.

On price, too, you will find that the Californian wines hold their own very well against many of the French, German and Italian varieties. Although the best European vintages are still considered generally superior, European table wines are more often than not vastly inferior to their Californian counterparts. Indeed, some of the local sparkling wines are world class.

In restaurants and bars you can order wine by the glass or carafe, as well as by the bottle. If you go to an unlicensed restaurant it is perfectly ac-

ceptable to take along your own bottle of wine.

Wine may be the most popular drink in California, but there are plenty of alternatives. One of Mexico's great gifts to America is **tequila**, best drunk in cocktail form as a Margarita – iced tequila with Cointreau or Triple Sec, lime juice, and a frosting of salt around the rim of the glass.

Europeans will find American **beers** are similar to European lagers, though slightly weaker. San Francisco is famous for its Anchor Steam beer, locally produced in a small brewery. Many foreign beers are served too, such as the Mexican Bohemia, Corona and Dos Equis – all excellent.

If you want to avoid alcohol, you can always order a variety of **fresh fruit juices** or a **mineral water**, a favourite of health-conscious Californians. Don't forget that California is rivalled only by Florida as the land of the orange. Demand it freshly squeezed, drink it by the gallon, and you just might begin to look like a Californian yourself.

BLUEPRINT
for a
Perfect Trip

An A–Z Summary of Practical Information

> Certain information in this section will be familiar to US residents, but has been included to help visitors from overseas.

A

ACCOMMODATION (See also CAMPING on p.119, the list of RECOMMENDED HOTELS on p.65, and YOUTH HOSTELS on p.141)

It is best to make advance hotel reservations in Los Angeles and San Francisco, even if you are travelling off-season. You can obtain a list of accommodation from the local Visitor Information Center (see p.140). For information on lodging in California's state and national parks, see CAMPING on p.119.

Motels are one of America's great bargains. Many belong to national (or even international) chains, so you can make all the bookings for your trip at the same time. They range in style from cheap basic rooms to luxury accommodation.

Bed-and-Breakfast establishments are becoming increasingly popular in California, but they are much more expensive than their counterparts in Europe. The California Office of Tourism publishes information on some 200 properties in their brochure *California Bed-and-Breakfast Inns*.

AIRPORTS

Los Angeles is served by Los Angeles International Airport (LAX) and Burbank Airport. All international and most domestic flights land at LAX, with Burbank Airport duplicating some of the short-hop flights. At Los Angeles International you'll find currency-exchange offices, snack bars, car-hire agencies and duty-free shops.

A 24-hour minibus service called Super Shuttle provides transport from LAX to points throughout Los Angeles. For information, tel.

338 1111. A transfer service from LAX to Burbank Airport is provided by Valley Airport Shuttle, tel. (818) 840 8847. A free shuttle bus takes passengers to the less expensive public bus terminal (RTD – Southern California Rapid Transit District) just outside the airport.

Taxis can be found at taxi stands outside each LAX terminal. The trip into town takes approximately 30 minutes, longer during peak traffic hours. Your hotel may provide a free limousine service for transportation into the city – inquire at the airport.

San Francisco is served by San Francisco International Airport (SFO), about 15 miles (26km) south of the city. The airport has currency exchange offices, restaurants, cocktail lounges, car-rental agencies and duty-free shops.

The SFO Airporter bus provides a frequent, non-stop service between the airport, Union Square and the Financial District – tel. 495 8404 for information. A Super Shuttle minibus service runs between the airport and any location in San Francisco, tel. 558 8500. Many hotels offer a free limousine service into town. The trip to the city centre takes between 20 and 40 minutes, depending on the traffic.

San Diego International Airport (Lindbergh Field) lies 3 miles (5km) north west of downtown San Diego. Transit bus 2 connects the airport with downtown, tel. 619 231 2100 for information. Alternatively, taxis are readily available outside the terminals.

Domestic flights. Air travel is by far the quickest and most convenient way of getting around the US. The most-travelled routes (eg LA–San Francisco) have shuttle services, where no advance booking is required. Travellers from abroad have the opportunity to buy in advance a Visit USA ticket, which provides discounted internal flights and sets no fixed programme. To benefit from these reduced-price tickets you must buy them prior to your arrival in the USA.

C

CAMPING
Camping is an excellent way to explore California's great outdoors. Most campsites are within the regional, state and national parks.

Facilities range from basic sites for tents only, with no amenities, to drive-in sites with all mod cons and hook-ups for RVs and trailers. Accommodation in the most popular parks must be booked through the park authority. If you want to hike overnight in the back country, you must first obtain a wilderness permit from the park headquarters. Camping on unofficial sites is illegal in most places in California.

If you want to drive around California you might consider the large motor caravans called RVs (recreational vehicles). They sleep from two to six people and can be hired for around $500 a week, though the best rates are available with package deals arranged through travel agents. Special RV campsites are listed in the California RV Park and Campground Guide, available from the California Travel Parks Association, PO Box 5648, Auburn, CA 95604.

Many campsites (such as Yosemite Valley) require reservations at least eight weeks in advance. Reservations for state parks can be made by dialling the MISTIX agency, tel. 800 444 7275.

For more information, contact the USTTA or the California Office of Tourism (see TOURIST INFORMATION OFFICES on p.140), or write to the California Department of Parks and Recreation, Publications Dept, PO. Box 942896, Sacramento, CA 94296, tel. (916) 653 6995. For information on national parks, contact the National Park Service, Building 201, Fort Mason, San Francisco, CA 94123, tel. (415) 556 0160.

CAR RENTAL (See also DRIVING on p.125)

The minimum age requirement varies from 18 to 25, but 21 is usual. You will need a full driver's licence, your passport, and a major credit card – cash deposits are not normally acceptable. Rates vary considerably, and you should shop around for the lowest price. The best rates are usually to be had by booking and paying for your car before you leave home, either directly through the UK office of an international rental company or as part of a fly-drive package. Check that the quoted rate includes collision damage waiver, unlimited mileage, and local sales tax, as these can considerably increase the cost. Minimum third-party cover of $1,000,000 is recommended.

CHILDREN'S CALIFORNIA

For children, California is one giant playground. Apart from the obvious attractions of Disneyland, Universal Studios and other theme parks, there are a hundred and one ways to entertain the youngsters. Here are a few suggestions:

Los Angeles: spend a day at the beach, though you should keep an eye on young children if there's any surf – there are good family beaches at Santa Monica, Marina del Rey, Dockweiler, and Dana Harbor in Orange County; hire a sailboat or motorboat at Fisherman's Village for a trip around Marina del Rey; ride the carousel and bumper cars on Santa Monica Pier; go and gawk at the mastodons in the George C Page Museum at the La Brea Tar Pits; enjoy the interactive exhibits at the LA Children's Museum downtown; hire some bicycles and go for a spin along the beachfront cycle-path; or learn about the stars (the heavenly, not the Hollywood, variety) at the Planetarium in the Griffith Observatory.

San Francisco: enjoy a hands-on introduction to science and technology at the Exploratorium; take a trip on a cable-car, or a switchback ride down the 'Crookedest Street in the World' (Lombard); watch the clowns and jugglers at Fisherman's Wharf, and explore the inside of a submarine at the USS *Pampanito*, before pigging out on chocolate at Ghirardelli Square; or take a drive down the coast to see the sea otters and tide-pool creatures in the Monterey Bay Aquarium.

San Diego: visit the animals at the world-famous San Diego Zoo, or go and see the killer whale and dolphins at Sea World; or in winter, try to spot some whales in their natural habitat from the whale-watching lookout at Point Loma; relax on the beach at Mission Bay; shake hands with a starfish at the Stephen Birch Aquarium in La Jolla; watch the hang-gliders and radio-control aeroplanes soaring and diving at the Torrey Pines Glider Park, just north of La Jolla; or cruise the toy shops in Horton Plaza, then delve into an ice-cream sundae in the open-air café on the top floor.

CLIMATE

The climate in California varies considerably from place to place. Southern California basks in a balmy, Mediterranean climate, but **121** unfortunately Los Angeles is prone to smog, and in June and July can be very foggy. The desert areas of Mojave and Death Valley inland are blisteringly hot in summer – often soaring above 100°F (38°C). Autumn to spring is the best time to visit these hot spots.

San Francisco is cooler and wetter, and in June and July, like LA, it's foggy almost every day. The sunniest months are August to October, the wettest December to February. The Sierra Nevada mountains suffer heavy snowfalls in winter, blocking roads.
Monthly average maximum daytime temperatures:

		J	F	M	A	M	J	J	A	S	O	N	D
Los Angeles	°C	18	19	20	22	23	25	28	29	28	25	23	19
	°F	64	66	68	72	74	77	82	84	82	77	74	66
San Francisco	°C	13	15	16	17	17	19	18	18	21	20	17	14
	°F	55	59	61	62	63	66	65	65	69	68	63	57

CLOTHING

In southern California most people dress all year round in comfortable, casual, lightweight clothes. Only the ritziest restaurants expect men to wear a jacket and tie. If you are visiting the northern part of the state, be prepared for cooler weather and rain in the winter, and pack a warm sweater and a raincoat. Don't forget a good pair of walking shoes in San Francisco for negotiating all those hills!

COMPLAINTS

If you have a serious complaint, and have talked with the manager of the establishment in question without success, try calling the California Consumer Complaint and Protection, tel. 800 952 5225, a toll-free number that can be called from anywhere in California.

CONSULATES

All embassies are in Washington DC.

CONSULATES IN LOS ANGELES:
Australia: 611 N Larchmont Boulevard, tel. (213) 469 4300, open 10am-3pm, Monday to Friday.

Canada: 300 S Grand Avenue, tel. (213) 687 7432, open 9am-4.30pm, Monday to Friday.

Germany: 6222 Wilshire Boulevard, Fifth floor, tel. (213) 930 2703, open 8-11.30am, Monday to Friday.

New Zealand: 10960 Wilshire Boulevard, tel. (310) 477 8241, open 9am-5pm, Monday to Friday.

United Kingdom: 3701 Wilshire Boulevard, tel. (310) 477 3322, open 9am-5pm, Monday to Friday.

CONSULATES IN SAN FRANCISCO:

Australia: 1 Bush Street, 7th floor, tel. 362 6160, open 9am-4pm, Monday to Friday.

Canada: 50 Fremont Street, tel. 495 6021, open 9am-5pm, Monday to Friday.

Eire: 655 Montgomery Street, tel. 392 4214, open 9am-4pm, Monday to Friday.

United Kingdom: 1 Sansome Street, tel. 981 3030, open 9am-4pm, Monday to Friday; closed 1-2pm for lunch.

CRIME (See also POLICE on p.134)

You should take the usual precautions against theft – don't carry large amounts of cash, leave your valuables in the hotel safe, not in your room, and beware of pickpockets in crowded areas. Never leave your bags or valuables on view in a parked car – take them with you or lock them in the boot. Any theft or loss must be reported immediately to the police in order to comply with your travel insurance. If your passport is lost or stolen, you should also inform your consulate (see CONSULATES above).

Although the tourist areas in California's cities are quite safe, there are certain districts where visitors should take care after dark, such as downtown and Venice Beach in LA, and the Tenderloin (the triangle formed by Ellis, Hyde and Market streets) and Western Addition in San Francisco.

CUSTOMS and ENTRY FORMALITIES

For visits of up to 90 days, UK citizens need only a valid 10-year passport and a return ticket with an airline participating in the visa waiver scheme. Citizens of Ireland, Australia and New Zealand need a visitor's visa, which can be obtained at any US embassy or consulate – apply at least four weeks in advance. Canadians need only present proof of nationality. (Visa regulations change from time to time, and should be confirmed through your travel agent. Alternatively, call the US Embassy's Visa Information Line (in the UK) on 0891 200 290.) On arrival you must fill out a customs declaration form (usually distributed by your airline at the end of the flight).

The following chart shows items you may take into the US duty-free (if you are over 21) and, returning home, into your own country:

Into:	Cigarettes		Cigars		Tobacco	Spirits		Wine
USA	200	or	50g	or	1,350g	1l	or	1l
Australia	200	or	250g	or	250g	1l	or	1l
Canada	200	and	50g	and	900g	1.1l	or	1.1l
Eire	200	or	50g	or	250g	1l	and	2l
N. Zealand	200	or	50g	or	250g	1l	and	4.5l
S. Africa	400	and	50g	and	250g	1l	and	2l
UK	200	or	50g	or	250g	1l	and	2l

A non-resident may claim, free of duty and taxes, articles up to $100 in value for use as gifts for other people. The exemption is valid only if the gifts accompany you, if you stay 72 hours or more and have not claimed this exemption within the preceding six months. Up to 100 cigars may be included within this gift exemption.

Plants and foodstuffs are also subject to strict control; visitors from abroad may not import fruits, vegetables or meat. The same goes for chocolates containing liqueurs.

Currency restrictions. Arriving and departing passengers should report any money, cheques, banker's drafts etc, exceeding a total of

$10,000.

DISABLED TRAVELLERS

State law requires that all new buildings provide wheelchair access and special restrooms, and pavements are easily negotiated by wheelchair. Most public transport has been modified to allow easy access, and staff are trained to assist. Information both on access and facilities can be obtained from the following sources:

Los Angeles County Commission on Disabilities, 383 Hall of Administration, 500 W Temple Street, Los Angeles, CA 90012, tel. (213) 974 1053.

Disability Co-ordinator, Mayor's Office of Community Development, 10 United Nations Plaza (Suite 600), San Francisco, CA 94102, tel. (415) 554 8925.

Accessible San Diego, 2466 Bartell Street, San Diego, CA 92123, tel. (619) 279 0704.

DRIVING

Driving conditions. California was designed around the car, and driving conditions are generally excellent. However, in the major cities, and especially in LA, there is often bad traffic congestion, and driving during rush hour is best avoided.

Drive on the right-hand side of the road. Speed limits range from 30-35mph (50-55kph) in all built-up areas, and is 55mph (90kph) on all highways except freeways where it is normally 65mph (105kph). Freeways are like British motorways, but there is no fast lane as such – cars cruise where they like – and overtaking on the inside is quite common. Note that trucks are not allowed to use the outside lane, so do not impede them by hogging the centre lane. Drink-driving is a very serious offence, and it is illegal even to carry an opened container of alcohol in the car. The wearing of seat belts is compulsory.

In California it is legal to make a right-hand turn at a red light provided that the road is clear and you have given way to any pedestrians. At city crossroads a common feature is the four-way stop **125** sign. Here you must come to a complete halt, and give way to any vehicle that arrived at the intersection before you. If there is a queue of cars they take turns to cross. Watch out for the bright yellow school buses. When a school bus has stopped with red lights flashing, traffic in both directions must stop too. In San Francisco cablecars have right of way over other road users.

Parking. In the cities, parking facilities consist mostly of meters and underground or multi-storey car-parks (parking lot). If you park on the street, pay close attention to the signs. Parking restrictions are rigorously enforced, and your car could be ticketed or towed away – a costly procedure. A red-painted kerb means no parking at any time, a rule that also applies a few yards either side of a fire hydrant. If you are leaving your car overnight, watch for signs that prohibit parking on certain days for early-morning street cleaning. When using a shopping mall car-park be sure to have your ticket validated in a shop or restaurants, as this will entitle you to free parking. In San Francisco a car parked on a steep hill must have its front wheels turned into the kerb, so that if it rolls downhill the kerb will brake it.

Petrol (gas). Petrol is sold by the US gallon (four-fifths of an Imperial gallon), is very cheap compared to European prices, and is almost always unleaded. Service stations are numerous and easily located, and are usually self-service. Many are open 24 hours. In some stations you may have to pay first and then fill up.

Breakdown. If your car breaks down on the freeway, pull over, switch on your hazard warning lights, and raise the bonnet (hood). If there is an emergency telephone in sight, just pick up the receiver and the Highway Patrol will answer. If not, wait for a patrol car to come by and assist. If you have a rental car, follow the procedure laid down by the rental company – there will usually be a 24-hour emergency telephone number, and the company will arrange for repairs or a replacement.

Find out before you leave if your car insurance covers you away from home. Californian insurance companies offer short-term policies but at exorbitant rates. The American Automobile Association

(AAA) can arrange short-term insurance. Contact AAA World Wide Travel, 1000 AAA Drive, Heathrow, Florida, tel. 32746-5603.

Distances. Here are the road distances between some important places, plus approximate driving times:

San Diego–Los Angeles	118 miles (190km)	2½ hours
Los Angeles–San Francisco	425 miles (684km)	9 hours
San Francisco–Yosemite	193 miles (310km)	4¼ hours
Los Angeles–Sequoia National Park	227 miles (365km)	5 hours
Los Angeles–Tijuana, Mexico	135 miles (217km)	2½ hours
Los Angeles–Las Vegas	284 miles (457km)	6 hours

Fluid measures

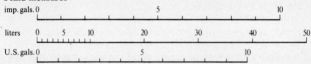

Distance

E

ELECTRIC CURRENT
110 V/60 Hz AC is standard throughout the USA. Plugs are two-pin, flat-pronged. European electrical appliances will need an adapter and a 240–110V transformer.

EMERGENCIES
In an emergency situation, dial **911** for police, fire or ambulance services, and an operator will connect you to the service you require.

ETIQUETTE

It's an egalitarian society in California, so you'll have to get used to American informality. Don't be startled if a new acquaintance calls you by your first (given) name, or starts asking intimate questions. Certain elements of politeness are pronounced throughout the state, such as the American use of 'Sir' or 'Ma'am', even when summoning a waiter or waitress. 'Thank you' is answered by 'you're welcome' or 'you're quite welcome' where 'quite' means 'very'.

GETTING TO CALIFORNIA

FROM GREAT BRITAIN

By Air: The major carriers offer daily non-stop flights from Heathrow to Los Angeles, San Diego and San Francisco. Average flying time to the West Coast is 11 hours. Fares available include First Class, Economy, Super-APEX , Special Economy and Standby. Super-APEX must be booked 21 days before travel for a stay of 7 to 180 days. Children fly for two-thirds of the Super-APEX fare. Special Economy fares can be booked at any time and offer plenty of flexibility. Standby fares are bookable only on the day of travel, minimum 2 hours prior to departure.

Some US airlines offer travellers from abroad a discount on internal flights, or flat-rate, unlimited-travel tickets. You must buy these tickets before you arrive in the USA.

Charter Flights and Package Tours: Many operators advertise holidays featuring Los Angeles and/or San Francisco, with excursions to Las Vegas, Yosemite, the Grand Canyon, etc. Fly-drive packages can be arranged through tour operators and certain airlines. Check with a travel agent for the latest deals.

FROM NORTH AMERICA

By Air: Direct flights connect over 100 American and Canadian cities to Los Angeles, San Diego and San Francisco every day. As these routes are highly competitive, special fares are readily available and prices change frequently. The Super Saver fare must be booked and paid for 30 days in advance. Children fly for two-thirds of this fare. Most airlines sell round-trip Excursion tickets, requiring payment at least seven days before travel. Fly-drive vacations, including flight, hotel and car rental, are offered by many airlines.

By Bus: California destinations are served by Greyhound bus. Passengers can make as many stopovers as they like, provided they reach their destination before their ticket expires. Visitors from abroad can buy an Ameripass from a travel agent in their home country. These tickets offer unlimited coach travel for a specified period – 4, 7, 15 or 30 days. Sightseeing coach tours, including accommodation, are also available.

By Train: Los Angeles and San Francisco are linked to most of the major cities in the USA and Canada by Amtrak rail services. Reduced fares are offered on a range of popular routes, such as Chicago–Los Angeles. Amtrak offers a variety of bargain fares, including Excursion and Family fares, USA Rail Passes, and tour packages with hotel and guide included.

By Car: The main Interstate freeways leading to California are the I-10 from Jacksonville, Florida, which runs along the southern edge of the USA through Houston and Phoenix to Los Angeles; the I-70 from New York and the Midwest, which leads via Denver to the I-15 and then to Los Angeles; and the I-80 from Chicago and Salt Lake City to San Francisco. The I-5 runs along the West Coast from Vancouver and Seattle to San Diego. The I-5 and the I-80 north and east of San Francisco may be briefly blocked by winter snows between October and April.

GUIDES and TOURS

Your nearest Visitor Information Center (see TOURIST INFORMATION OFFICES on p.140) can give you a list of agencies offering organized city tours and excursions. Guided tours are offered at some major attractions, such as Hearst Castle and Universal Studios and are part of the admission fee.

LANGUAGE

Divided by a common language, below are some of the most common Anglo-American misunderstandings:

US	British	US	British
bill	banknote	**liquor**	spirits
check	bill (restaurant)	**pants**	trousers
collect call	reverse-charge call	**purse**	handbag
elevator	lift	**second floor**	first floor
faucet	tap	**subway**	underground
first floor	ground floor	**suspenders**	braces
gas(oline)	petrol	**underpass**	subway

LAUNDRY and DRY CLEANING

If you are staying in a hotel it may offer a laundry and dry-cleaning service, but it is usually less expensive to seek out a local launderette, some of which have armchairs, coffee machines and TV.

LOST PROPERTY

Air, rail and bus terminals and many department stores and shopping malls have special 'lost-and-found' departments. If your lost property is valuable, contact the police. If you lose your passport, get in touch with your consulate immediately (see CONSULATES on p.122).

M

MAPS

You can pick up free maps and brochures at any Visitor Information Center (see TOURIST INFORMATION OFFICES on p.140), and at National Park Visitor Centers. Excellent city and state maps can be bought for a few dollars in bookshops and petrol (gas) stations.

MEDICAL CARE

Make sure you take out adequate medical insurance before leaving home. The USA does not provide free medical care, and a visit to the doctor or a stay in hospital can prove very expensive. Vaccinations are not required for visitors arriving from Europe.

If you need a doctor, your hotel should be able to recommend one. Alternatively, contact the Los Angeles County Medical Association, tel. (213) 483 6122, or the San Francisco Medical Society, tel. (415) 561 0853. If you need a dentist, call the Southern California Dental Referral Service, tel. 800 235 4111.

A prescription is required for most medicines, which can be obtained at any local pharmacy. Also known as drugstores, pharmacies are usually open seven days a week and many offer delivery service.

MONEY MATTERS

Currency. The unit of currency is the dollar ($), divided into 100 cents (¢). Banknotes come in $1, $2 (rare), $5, $10, $20, $50 and $100 denominations. All notes are the same size and colour, so be sure to check them before you hand them over. Coins are 1¢ (penny), 5¢ (nickel), 10¢ (dime), 25¢ (quarter), 50¢ (half dollar) and $1.

Banks and currency exchange offices. Banks are generally open 10am-3pm Monday to Thursday and until 5 or 6pm on Friday. Larger ones will change foreign money and foreign-currency traveller's cheques. San Francisco and Los Angeles international airports have currency exchange offices open daily 7am-11pm. In Los Angeles you can change money at Continental Currency Services at 6565 Hollywood Boulevard, open 24 hours Monday to Saturday. In San Francisco, Macy's department store on Union Square has a currency exchange office open 9.30am-9pm on weekdays, 9.30am-6pm on Saturday and 12-5pm on Sunday.

Travellers' cheques and credit cards. American dollar travellers' cheques are universally accepted as cash in hotels, restaurants and shops. Travellers' cheques in a foreign currency must be exchanged at a major bank. The major credit cards are accepted almost everywhere, and are particularly useful for renting a car or making a hotel reservation by phone. Credit cards can also be used with a PIN to obtain a dollar cash advance from Automatic Teller Machines (ATMs).

Sales tax. A sales tax (currently 8.25%) is added to the price of all goods (except unprepared food) purchased in California. Taxes are also levied on hotel and motel prices (see also p.65).

NEWSPAPERS and MAGAZINES

The main West Coast dailies are the *San Francisco Chronicle*, the *San Francisco Examiner* and the well-respected *Los Angeles Times*. All produce a weekend listings section with details of local cinema, theatre, music and events. You can find European newspapers a day or two old at specialist downtown news-stands.

OPENING HOURS

Banks are generally open 10am-3pm Monday to Thursday and until 5pm or 6pm Friday, closed weekends.

Post offices open 9am-5pm Monday to Friday, to 1pm on Saturday.

Shops. Retail stores are usually open 9.30am-6pm Monday to Saturday. Most department stores stay open until 9 pm at least once a week and some are open on Sunday afternoon. Many supermarkets and drugstores stay open 24 hours, seven days a week. Shops in malls are usually open late seven days a week.

San Francisco area sightseeing:
Alcatraz. 9.30am-4.15pm daily, until 2.45pm in winter.
Coit Tower. 9am-4.30pm daily.
Golden Gate Park. M H de Young and Asian Art Museums, 10am-5pm Wednesday to Sunday. California Academy of Sciences 10am-5pm daily, later in summer. Japanese Tea Garden 8am-dusk daily.

Palace of the Legion of Honor. Closed until April 1994, but normally open 10am-5pm daily.
Exploratorium. 10am-5pm Tuesday to Sunday.
Fort Point National Historic Site. 10am-5pm every day except Christmas Day.

Los Angeles area sightseeing:
Disneyland. 9am-midnight daily in summer (19 June to Labor Day); 10am-6pm Wednesday to Friday and 9am-midnight on Saturday and Sunday in winter.
Farmers Market. 9am-7pm Monday to Saturday, and 10am-6pm Sunday.
Huntington Library. 1-4.30pm Tuesday to Sunday.
J Paul Getty Museum. 10am-5pm Tuesday to Sunday year-round. Parking reservations required one week in advance.
Knott's Berry Farm. 10am-6pm Monday, Tuesday and Friday; 10am-10pm Saturday and 10am-8pm Sunday.
Norton Simon Museum. Noon-6 pm Thursday to Sunday.
Queen Mary. 10.30am-4pm daily (6pm in summer).
Universal Studios. 8.30am-10pm summer, 9am-6.30pm in winter.

P

PHOTOGRAPHY and VIDEO
All well-known brands of film are available as are inexpensive 1-hour or overnight processing for colour print film. Blank video tape is available for all types of camera, but note that pre-recorded tapes for the US market won't work on European systems.

PLANNING YOUR BUDGET
To give you an idea of what to expect, here's a list of prices in US dollars. These should be regarded as approximate, as inflation continues to push prices up.
Airport transfers. From LAX to Hollywood or downtown Los Angeles by airport shuttle bus $12; by taxi $25. From SFO International to downtown San Francisco by airport bus $8; by taxi $25.

Camping. Tents: developed sites $12-16 a night; wilderness sites free-$7 a night. Trailer (caravan) and RV hook-ups: $16-40 a night.

Car rental. As a rough guide, expect to pay around $30-40 a day and $170-200 a week for an economy/compact model, including tax, collision damage waiver and unlimited mileage.

Entertainment. Cinema $4-7; theatre $15-20; concerts $10-30; nightclub cover charge $8-12.

Excursions. Cruise to Catalina from Long Beach $28.50 round trip; coach trip from Monterey to Hearst Castle $45; whale-watching boat trips from San Francisco $40.

Hotels (double room with bath). Motel or budget hotel $30-70; middle-range hotel $70-125; de luxe hotel $125-300.

Meals and drinks. Full breakfast in diner $5-7; lunch in coffee shop $7; dinner in restaurant from $15 up. Coffee $1; soft drinks $1; wine from $9 a bottle; beer $2 a glass.

Public transport. In San Francisco: MUNI buses and streetcars $1 flat fare; cable-cars $3 flat fare; seven-day pass $15; BART trains $2.60; ferry to Sausalito $3.50 one-way. In Los Angeles: RTD buses $1.10 basic fare; downtown DASH buses $0.25; Metro $1.10 flat fare. In San Diego: bus from $1.25; trolley $0.50-2.25.

Sightseeing. Museums and art galleries $2-6; theme parks $20 and up; Universal Studios, Disneyland $29.00 adult, $23.00 child; Alcatraz, including self-guided audio tour, $12; Hearst Castle guided tour $14; National Parks entrance fee $5 per vehicle.

Taxis. $1.90 basic fare plus $1.60 a mile.

POLICE

Theft and other crimes should be reported to the police department of the city in which they occurred. This procedure is necessary if you are going to make an insurance claim. In an emergency dial **911** and ask for the police. For non-urgent matters, use the following numbers: San Francisco Police Department, tel. (415) 553 0123; Los Angeles City Hall, tel. (213) 485 2121, or Los Angeles Police Department, tel. (213) 626 5273.

The freeways are policed by the California Highway Patrol (nicknamed CHIPS). They can be contacted through the emergency telephones located along the main highways, or phone (213) 736 3374.

POST OFFICES

Post office hours are 9am-5pm Monday to Friday and 9am-1pm on Saturday, although some branches have longer hours. Mail boxes are blue and are usually located on street corners.

General delivery (poste restante). If you don't know in advance where you'll be staying, you can have your mail addressed to you, c/o General Delivery, Metropolitan Station, 901 South Broadway, Los Angeles, CA 90014 (they require advance notice), or c/o General Delivery, Main Post Office, Seventh and Mission streets, San Francisco, CA 94101. Your mail will be held for 30 days.

American Express will also hold mail for visitors (without charge if you hold their travellers' cheques or credit card): c/o American Express, 723 W 7th Street, Los Angeles, CA 90017; or c/o American Express, 237 Post Street, San Francisco, CA 94111.

Telegrams and faxes. Telegraph services in the US are privately run and are not handled by the post office. You can call a telegraph office (check the YELLOW PAGES) from your hotel room, dictate your message, and have the charge added to your hotel bill, or dictate it from a coin-operated phone and pay on the spot. You can send faxes from most hotels as well as from photocopying shops.

PUBLIC HOLIDAYS

Banks, government offices and many businesses close on the following holidays, or on the nearest Monday or Friday. Thanksgiving is a major holiday which lasts from Thursday to Sunday.

1 January	*New Year's Day*
Third Monday in January	*Martin Luther King Day*
Third Monday in February	*Presidents' Day*
(moveable date)	*Easter Monday*
Last Monday in May	*Memorial Day*

4 July	*Independence Day*
First Monday in September	*Labor Day*
Second Monday in October	*Columbus Day*
11 November	*Veterans' Day*
Last Thursday in November	*Thanksgiving Day*
25 December	*Christmas Day*

PUBLIC TRANSPORT

San Francisco and the Bay Area are served by a cheap and efficient network of buses, streetcars, cable-cars, ferries and the BART subway. The buses and streetcars are run by MUNI (Municipal Railways) and serve the entire metropolitan area. For information, call 673-MUNI, or pick up route maps at the Visitor Information Center (see TOURIST INFORMATION OFFICES on p.140). Multi-day passes for unlimited travel are available.

The BART (Bay Area Rapid Transit System) subway links San Francisco with the East Bay area. Trains run from 4-12am Monday to Friday, 6-12am Saturday and 8-12am Sunday. Route maps are located in the stations and on the trains. You buy your flat-fare ticket from a coin-operated machine. For information, dial 788-BART.

Other bus services cover the communities outside central San Francisco. A/C Transit (tel. 839 2882) serves the East Bay Area, Sam Trans (tel. 800 660-4BUS) covers the Bay Area south to Palo Alto, and Golden Gate Transit (tel. 332 6600) covers Marin and Sonoma Counties via the Golden Gate Bridge.

Ferries to Tiburon, Alcatraz and Angel Island depart from Fisherman's Wharf (tel. 546-BOAT). Boats to Sausalito leave from the Ferry Building at the end of Market Street (tel. 332 6600).

Los Angeles. The urban sprawl of LA is more difficult to negotiate by public transport. The majority of the buses are run by RTD (Southern California Rapid Transit District). For information dial 626 4455. Santa Monica Municipal Bus Lines serve West Los Angeles, Santa Monica, Malibu, Pacific Palisades, Venice and Marina del Rey areas (tel. 451 5444). Downtown is served by the DASH shuttle bus, with buses every 6-15 minutes (tel. 800 2LA-RIDE).

A light-rail network (Metro) run by RTD is currently under construction, which will eventually link the downtown area with the outlying suburbs. The Blue Line to Long Beach, and the Red Line to Wilshire and Seventh, are already in operation, with trains every ten minutes, from 5am-7pm (tel. 626 4455).

Regular ferries run from San Pedro and Long Beach to Catalina Island. For schedules and rates, call Catalina Express (tel. (310) 519 1212), or Catalina Cruises (tel. (213) 253 9800, or 800-CATALINA).

San Diego has an excellent network of bus and tram services. San Diego Transit runs the buses – for information, tel. 233 3004. The tram service, known as the Trolley, runs all the way to Tijuana at the Mexican border (tel. 231 8549). To pick up route maps and timetables, or to buy a Day Tripper Transit Pass, call in at the Transit Store, 449 Broadway, tel. 234 1060.

R

RADIO and TV

Your hotel or motel room will almost certainly have a TV, with a range of up to 30 channels, plus cable TV. All national networks, ABC, CBS and NBC, have hour-long early-evening news programmes. PBS shows documentaries, drama and quality programmes – no commercials. Cable channels include one with non-stop movies, CNN (24-hour news) and MTV (pop music videos). Newspapers provide full details (see NEWSPAPERS AND MAGAZINES on p.132).

The airwaves are also crammed with radio stations, featuring everything from rock to reggae, country to classical, along with chat shows, religious programmes and sports coverage. A special waveband carries recorded information on national and state parks.

RELIGIOUS SERVICES

All the major religious denominations are represented in California. To find the nearest place of worship, ask at the local Visitor Information Center (see p.141), or check the phone book. Saturday newspapers often list services for the following day.

TAXIS

You can pick up a taxi at one of the ranks at airports, railway stations, bus terminals and major hotels, but if you try hailing one in the street the odds are it won't stop. It's better to get your hotel to order one by phone, or call one yourself.

Fares are clearly displayed inside the cab, along with the driver's name and number (in case of complaints). A tip of at least 15 percent is expected. In Los Angeles, remember that the large distances involved can make travelling by taxi an expensive business.

TELEPHONES

The US telephone service is provided by a number of private companies, such as AT&T, MCI, and Sprint. There are two kinds of public telephone – coin-operated and credit-card. Local, long-distance, international and collect (reverse-charge) calls can be made from any phone – instructions are posted in the phone booth. For calls outside the local area, first dial 1, then the area code and number. Coin-operated pay phones accept 5, 10 and 25¢ coins – minimum charge for a local call is 25¢. For long distance, dial the number and you will be told the minimum charge. To use a credit-card telephone, simply 'wipe' your card through the slot as instructed, and dial as usual.

To call direct to the UK, first call the operator to find out how much money to insert, then dial 011 44, followed by the UK local dialling code (without the initial zero), and the number. The operator will intercept when more coins are needed. To make a reverse charge or BT Chargecard call, dial 1 800 445 5667 (AT&T phones only), which puts you through direct to an operator in the UK.

Many services and businesses have a toll-free number, beginning with the code 800, which you can call for no charge from anywhere in the USA (dial 1 first, as for long distance). American telephones also have letters as well as numbers on the keypad, and many commercial numbers are given as easily remembered words.

Operator	0
International operator	00 (AT&T phones)
Local directory enquiries	411
Long-distance directory enquiries	1 area code 555 1212

TIME DIFFERENCES

California is on Pacific Standard Time, which is GMT minus eight hours. In summer (April–October) Daylight Saving Time is adopted and clocks are moved forward one hour. To find out the exact time in Los Angeles, dial 853 1212; in San Francisco, dial 767 8900.

In the US, dates are written in the order month/day/year. For example, 2/4/99 is 4 February 1999. The following chart shows time differences between California and various other locations in winter:

California	Chicago	New York	London	Sydney
noon	2pm	3pm	8pm	7am
Sunday	Sunday	Sunday	Sunday	Monday

TIPPING

Service is not usually included in the bill, and you must tip your waiter, waitress or bartender 15-20 percent (more if service is exceptional). Hotel staff, guides and taxi drivers should also be tipped.

TOILETS

Public toilets are located in airports, bus and railway terminals, museums, department stores, restaurants and petrol (gas) stations. The terms 'rest-room' or 'bathroom' rather than toilet are generally used.

TOURIST INFORMATION OFFICES

If you want general information on California while planning your trip, contact one of the offices listed below.

In the UK: United States Travel and Tourism Administration, PO Box 1EN, London W1A 1EN, tel. (071) 495 4466.

In the US: California Office of Tourism, 801 K Street (Suite 1600), Sacramento, CA 95814, tel. 916 322 288.

Here are the main Visitor Information Centers:

San Francisco Visitor Information Center, Lower Level, Hallidie Plaza, 900 Market Street (between Powell and Mason streets), tel. (415) 391 2000. Open 9am-5.30pm Monday to Friday, 9am-3pm Saturday, 10am-2pm Sunday. For 24-hour recorded information on daily events and activities, telepone (415) 391 2001. Write to the San Francisco Convention and Visitors Bureau, PO Box 429097, San Francisco, CA 94142 9097.

Los Angeles Convention and Visitors Bureau operates two Visitor Information Centers – downtown, at 695 S Figueroa Street (between Wilshire Boulevard and Seventh Street), open 8am-5pm Monday to Saturday; and in Hollywood, at The Janes House, Janes Square, 6541 Hollywood Boulevard, open 9am-5pm Monday to Saturday. Tel. (213) 689 8822. Write to the Los Angeles Convention and Visitors Bureau, 515 S Figueroa Street (Suite 1100), Los Angeles, CA 90017.

San Diego International Visitor Information Center, First Avenue at F Street, 11 Horton Plaza, tel. (619) 236 1212. Open daily 8.30am-5pm except Thanksgiving and Christmas Day, 11am-5pm Sunday. Write to the San Diego Convention and Visitors Bureau, 1200 Third Avenue (Suite 824), San Diego, CA 92101-4190.

WATER

California's tap water is perfectly safe to drink. However, the state suffers from a chronic water shortage, and visitors are encouraged to help by following a number of simple water conservation measures – take showers instead of baths, and avoid letting the tap run while brushing your teeth, shaving, or washing your hands.

If you are camping in the wilder areas of the national parks, do not drink water from streams or rivers unless it has been boiled for at least 5 minutes or treated with water-purifying tablets.

WEIGHTS and MEASURES

For fluid and distance measures see DRIVING on p.127

Temperature

Length

Weight

grams, ounces

Y

YOUTH HOSTELS

The American Youth Hostels Association (AYH) runs a number of
hostels throughout California. Most of them are in hiking areas, but
there are a few in San Francisco, Los Angeles and San Diego. A
dorm bed costs $9-15 a night for AYH and IYHF members, a few
more dollars for non-members. You can join on the spot by paying
the membership fee. Further information and a list of hostels in the
USA and worldwide are available from the AYH National Offices,
PO Box 37613, Washington DC 20013-7613, tel. (202) 783 6161, or
from the International Youth Hostel Federation (IYHF), 9 Guessens
Road, Welwyn Garden City, Herts AL8 6QW, United Kingdom, tel.
(0707) 332 487.

Index

Where more than one page reference is given, the one in **bold** is the main entry listed.